# Shadow of the
# Colossus

# Shadow of the Colossus

Nick Suttner

Boss Fight Books
Los Angeles, CA
bossfightbooks.com

ISBN 13: 978-1-940535-10-4
First Printing: 2015
Second Printing: 2016
Third Printing: 2019

Series Editor: Gabe Durham
Book Design by Ken Baumann
Page Design by Adam Robinson

*For Amber, my Mono*
*and Finn, my Agro*

# CONTENTS

# FOREWORD

WHEN I WAS GROWING UP, every so often I would stumble over a video game with a startling vision or a personal touch—where some deep video game magic was allowed to take root. In the early 2000s while at art school, I had a strong interest in creating my own games with these qualities. To this end I founded Superbrothers, began painting pixels and poking at prototypes.

I had been playing video games on VIC-20, Commodore 64, PC, and on Nintendo systems. I was late to PlayStation, but when I encountered Fumito Ueda's *Ico* I was floored. The characters seemed alive and the spaces felt real. There was none of the usual noise or dissonance. Instead there was a soul, a heartbeat.

When Fumito Ueda's next effort *Shadow of the Colossus* emerged a few years later, it was a memorable moment for myself and my housemates. We hooked it up to a projector and played it on the slanted wall looming over our living room attic. It was dazzling!

*Shadow*'s scope and spectacle were unprecedented, but then there was that stoic sadness—that lingering weirdness, those mysterious whispers, those touches of darkness and wonderment… and within was that quiet warmth, gradually eroding. It was a potent brew.

After my encounter with *Shadow*, I spent a few years at a traditional Japanese video game company in Toronto before I met the folks at Capy Games and we began to build *Superbrothers: Sword & Sworcery EP* with a tiny team. In *Sworcery*'s credits we cited as inspirations Jordan Mechner, Eric Chahi… and, of course, Fumito Ueda.

*Sworcery* employs a cinematic, slightly handheld camera style. The design is fairly stripped-down, with touches of *The Legend of Zelda*. The story concept involves a sword-carrying protagonist traversing a mythic natural landscape, whose semi-obscure adventure is motivated by an unseen presence, and whose spirit degrades as the adventure wears on towards its grimly climactic finale. Echoes of *Shadow*, to be sure.

An unexpected highlight of my first trip to Japan while attending to *Sworcery*'s Japanese launch was a lengthy evening conversation with Fumito Ueda himself. We spoke mostly about the practicalities of creating video games with heart, and I was struck by how Ueda's warm, composed, precise, and sincere manner so perfectly matched the tone of his video games.

All these years later, *Shadow* still stands apart, casting into stark relief some of today's more muddled action-adventure games. For me, *Shadow* demonstrates that a video game can audaciously mount a cinematic spectacle with a bold concept and a distinctive style while simultaneously being understated, heartfelt, even intimate.

I think it's worth investigating *Shadow*'s particular profile, and you're in great hands here with Nick's wit, personal touches, deep appreciation, and profound insights.

Enjoy!
Craig D. Adams
founder/creator/bozo at Superbrothers A/V Inc.
Autumn, 2015

# INTRODUCTION

A MASSIVE, OPEN WORLD with almost nothing in it. A big-budget game that's more interested in exploring the experience of its questions than distracting you with answers. An unwavering trust that players will figure out where to go, what to do, and even think about *why* they're doing it. *Shadow of the Colossus* is a landmark in so many ways, and still unique more than a decade after its release.

It's also a study in focus, as it was in its time amongst its peers. *Resident Evil 4* released earlier that same year in 2005, revitalizing the entire survival-horror genre with a tight over-the-shoulder perspective that made combat a tense, precise nightmare. Just a couple of months later came *God of War*, a bold and bawdy exploration of Greek mythology with a deeply satisfying bloodlust.

All three games have since seen HD re-releases and are considered seminal events in gaming history. Yet both *Resident Evil 4* and *God of War* hew closely to convention, very much gamers' games filled with inventories, attack combos, and carefully scripted setpieces always upping the ante. Both games are also very filmic, with long expository cutscenes wrapped around every big event, and a monologue for every hero and villain that dives deeply into their lore.

Clearly, 2005 was an incredible year for games. But what interests me is just how far *Shadow* swung away from those other hits. Its reductions were across the board, and uncompromising: Only sixteen "enemies." Only two weapons, both of which you start with and will never level up. You'll never learn new moves, only strengthen your grip and your health over time. You won't unlock new areas, only new challenges in places that have been accessible all along. You won't meet any new main characters after the opening cinematic. There's (almost) nothing to collect.

Yet despite all that *isn't* there, *Shadow* is absolutely riveting. At a time when games were doubling down on the gamer by betting big on proven formulas, and leaning on the legacy of film to tell their stories, *Shadow* was content to spin its mystery up front and shove you into the blinding sun to fend for yourself and figure out the rest. The entirety of the experience lives deep within me, like some primordial dream. Soaring high above the sprawling desert, clinging to my foe as the wind laps at my unsteady feet. Finding the relief of fire at the bottom of a treacherous crevasse, itself in the shadow of an ancient, endless bridge.

• • • • • • • • • • • • • •

I first read about *Shadow* in the pages of *Electronic Gaming Monthly*, a long-running gaming magazine I would later write for. A game in which entire levels were puzzles set atop the backs of massive creatures, the promise of an epic puzzle-platformer from the team behind the thoughtful, sweetly haunting *Ico*. Building on their craft and artistry, Team Ico's *Shadow* promised action, and a gauntlet of giants to conquer. Its titular creatures were striking, even in those early screenshots. Towering, dimly sentient relics with piercing yellow eyes and mossy manes. I was smitten.

In broad strokes, *Shadow* is about a boy trying to save a girl. The situation is dire, and her last hope lies in a distant, long-abandoned corner of the world. He brings her to this place, throwing himself at the mercy of its overseer. This spirit tasks him with defeating a number of guardians that dwell within the land, and in exchange there may be a glimmer of hope for her yet.

But like so many wonderful moments in life and art, *Shadow of the Colossus* is defined by the space between its lines: the gulf between its quieter, contemplative moments and its tremendous spectacle. Strung end to end, its titanic battles would make for an amazing— if exhausting—barrage of action. But driving your horse across an imposing sunbaked expanse, twisting up through shade-mottled woods, only to find your ageless, unwitting foe at rest in the stillness of a lake gives the encounter exactly the breathing room it needs.

*Shadow* lets its best moments come to you at your own pace, subtly leading and showing rather than telling.

● ● ● ● ● ● ● ● ● ● ● ● ● ● ● ●

There were rumors that *Shadow* was originally planned to have whole cities and dungeons dotting its spartan landscapes, lost in time to schedules, or budgets, or something equally mundane. And one of the best, most wonderful things about it is that it *feels that way.* The remnants of a world that once was, or never was, frozen in time. A lost civilization perpetually under construction.

There are so many empty, functionally *useless* corners of *Shadow*'s expansive world, but it hurts to even call them that. They still feel alive and mysterious, as if exploring the right nook or climbing an especially precarious peak will unlock… something. A bridge to that lost civilization, a seventeenth colossus, some armor for my horse maybe. Despite its creator Fumito Ueda telling me years ago in an e-mail interview that all of *Shadow*'s secrets had been found, it never felt that way, and still doesn't.

Thankfully, the legacy and lessons of *Shadow* live on in gaming today, through a generation of fans, artists, and game developers—whose work carries its influence forward. Game development has become democratized in recent years through cheaper and more user-friendly software while the audience has expanded tremendously through more ubiquitous platforms to play on. As a result, many players are looking for more varied games across the full spectrum of human experience, and some of the themes that *Shadow* explored—such as hope, regret, and sacrifice—have become both easier and more commercially viable to express. At the same time, series such as Dark Souls have built on Team Ico's legacy, dropping players into vast, unforgiving worlds that seem to have existed long before they came along, with narratives that unfold primarily through the experience of gameplay rather than traditional storytelling—no doubt influencing a future generation of developers to live by the tenets of trusting and respecting their players while giving them something surreal and spectacular.

• • • • • • • • • • • • • • • •

Oh right, and I'm Nick Suttner, bearded indie game advocate. After writing about games for *EGM* and 1UP. com (where I hosted a retrospective podcast series on *Shadow*), I went to work at Sony to help shape the culture of independent games on PlayStation. *Shadow* is the entire reason I'm working in games, and specifically the reason I went to work at Sony (which published the game). I've spent almost nine years in the gaming industry championing the more artful, emotional, intellectually stimulating side of gaming, and truly, *Shadow* has been my constant muse.

My endeavor here as your guide, as a *Shadow* devotee, and as someone whose career and personal aesthetic has been so deeply influenced by the game, is to dig into the experience and unearth what makes it so special. Why is *Shadow* still so singular over a decade later? How has it managed to maintain an air of mystery beyond that of any other game? I'm hoping that you've played *Shadow* already, but if you haven't made time for it I'm happy to give you an excuse. Consider this your companion guide—I'll be playing through it again with a critical eye, talking about it with others who love it the way that I do, and sharing my findings along the way. Maybe I'll even pinpoint the enigmatic quality that grants the game it's enduring appeal. Or maybe not, and instead just get lost in the roar of the earth once again.

# ICO

BEFORE WE GO GALLOPING OFF across the plains of *Shadow of the Colossus*, it's important to look back at its genetic destiny—embodied in its deafeningly quiet predecessor *Ico*, humming just outside the periphery of gaming history. *Ico* (pronounced "EE-koh") released on the PlayStation 2 in September of 2001, engineered for uniqueness by an ambitious new team led by an imaginative young animator. While threads of companionship, fatalism, and futility would eventually weave their way through Team Ico's narratives, *Ico* started with a much simpler premise: a game about holding hands.

"The inspiration for *Ico* was to tell a story about a small boy and a taller girl," explains game director Fumito Ueda. "I just thought it would work really well visually, and that's how things got started. But you need more than that to make a game, so for the gameplay itself I had the idea of letting the player directly touch, interact with the AI."

Unlike many visionary creators, Ueda managed to largely skip the step of toiling away in obscurity before delivering what would later become recognized as his first seminal work. After graduating from Osaka University of Arts in 1993 he applied at game developer WARP, and despite not passing the initial application process he was hand-picked by company head Kenji Eno (who would later become an influential game composer before passing away in 2013) thanks to the concept behind some animation work Ueda had submitted of a dog running in the rain. He went on to work as an animator on their stealth horror game *Enemy Zero* during its brief, difficult development, before going to work at Sony Computer Entertainment in Tokyo in 1997. After working mostly by himself for a few months on a three-minute CG concept video for *Ico* (inspired in part by 1978 manga *Galaxy Express 999*), Ueda and his newly assigned producer Kenji Kaido were given the green light to move forward with production, though its development was kept under wraps for a number of years.

As best as I can remember, my first exposure to *Ico* was in the pages of *Official U.S. PlayStation Magazine (OPM)*, whose September 2001 cover proudly proclaimed it "The Best Game You've Never Heard Of"—something that still holds true today for many. Then-editor-in-chief John Davison remembers Sony being surprised that *OPM* wanted to put the game on the cover, scrambling just to provide the needed art assets. "We had opportunities to really champion games that we wanted to get behind," he told me via e-mail.

"Before *Ico*, we didn't know how to articulate the desire for a game experience that was defined by its artistic vision. It gave everyone something to point to and say 'something like that.' Fumito Ueda gave form to an aspiration."

Upon release, *Ico* was lauded for feeling like nothing else. "An ethereal and elusive opera," Ollie Barder of *The Guardian* would later call it—the most apt description I've found. The dreamlike adventure of a horned boy rescuing a pale girl from their castle-*cum*-prison, stripped of everything but the journey from point A to point B. With *Halo: Combat Evolved* and *Grand Theft Auto III* a month away from release, minimalism wasn't especially en vogue, but *Ico* stayed the course with a deft confidence that was hard not to notice. When most games still slotted neatly into a template of shooting, racing, or fighting, or iterating on our collective childhoods, Ueda had engineered a team to create something wonderfully undefinable. "Well, we didn't want to make a 'game-y' game from the start," explains Ueda, "so we felt that bringing in people who were entrenched in video games and the industry might be a problem, so we brought people in who didn't have a lot of experience [...] or from other areas like video production." I've read multiple interviews in which Ueda points to that same lack of experience—across almost the entire team, many of them friends of his from university—as the reason why they were able to avoid compromising their vision. They simply didn't know what they didn't know, and the sky was the limit.

● ● ● ● ● ● ● ● ● ● ● ● ● ● ● ●

As *Shadow* would do years later, *Ico* unfurls most of its story up front in a single, beautiful cutscene, economic in its intrigue. Masked men journey through an idyllic forest, escorting a young horned boy on horseback (whose name—Ico—we won't learn until the closing credits). They soon reach the edge of the forest, the decaying ruins of what used to be one end of a massive stone bridge set into a sheer cliff overlooking an ocean. Where the bridge would have found purchase on the other end, we see the walkways, ramps, and arches of a huge foreboding castle built into a rocky island outcropping.

Ico is carried, childlike, deep into the guts of the castle to a glowing stone pod, already open and eagerly awaiting its new prisoner, while dozens of other pods line the walls, standing still and silent. "Do not be angry with us," the men say as Ico is sealed inside. "This is for the good of the village." After they've left, the boy rattles the pod, which—almost too easily—falls and cracks apart, spilling him out into the cavernous room.

Ico moves with a loose, skidding awkwardness—as real boys do—animated with the misplaced confidence of adolescence. His movements are weighty and intuitive, driven by momentum. It's fun just moving him around. The adventure is framed from deliberate vantage points, with a non-traditional third-person camera that watches like an eye pinned to a different spot in each room, turning to look as Ico scurries by. The camera often accentuates the depth or scale of the spaces, creating expansive chambers and dizzying drops simply through clever positioning.

Another of Ico's visual experiments is the player's ability to move the camera during cutscenes to peek just offscreen, perhaps Ueda's nod to *Super Mario Bros.*, the game that convinced him that video games were a particularly intriguing medium: "It was the first game where I felt there was a world beyond what you could see on the screen," he told 1UP.com in 2011. "Up until then, you just kind of thought it ended with whatever you saw, but with Mario it felt like the world extended beyond that."

*Ico*'s transitions between cutscenes and gameplay are seamless—there's never any information or iconography displayed on screen, just a beautiful window into a lonely stone world for your adventures to take place in, undistracted. I can't think of many earlier games that kept the screen completely clear of extraneous information, save the 1991 Amiga classic *Another World* (known as *Out of This World* in North America), a cinematic adventure game set in a harrowing sci-fi world that's cited by Ueda as one of the key influences behind *Ico*. I spoke to its creator Eric Chahi via e-mail about his decision to keep the presentation so spartan in a time when games were anything but. "Having scores was standard at the time—it was the legacy of arcade games. But it was anti-immersive. It collided with the universe and distracted the player, so I intentionally decided to break the rules. One consequence of doing so is that life becomes infinite." Indeed, that small aesthetic innovation moved many games away from the concept of "lives," an increasingly unnecessary trope when you weren't pumping quarters into a machine, and one that's critical to *Ico*'s narrative momentum.

• • • • • • • • • • • • • • •

At the top of a huge, cylindrical room, Ico finds—and shortly frees—Yorda (whose name we also won't learn until the end), a pale girl trapped in a cage, dressed all in white. Yorda speaks in a strange tongue (depicted as hieroglyphs in the subtitles), and despite her fragile appearance, seems powerful. Otherworldly. Startled at times but never scared, curious but hesitant. And she's taller than Ico, as Ueda promised, a small but effective visual touch.

Ico tells her that all horned children are brought here. "Were they trying to sacrifice you too?" he asks in his own strange language (subtitled in English), a curious choice of words that we'll learn little else about. Interrupting them, a shadowy creature with glowing blue eyes tries to carry Yorda away, which Ico must beat back with a flaming stick. Even after it drops her and disappears, Yorda just sits there quietly, unfazed. This leads to the first of many beautiful gameplay interactions between the two. Pressing the R1 button reaches out to Yorda, lifting her to her feet, and will thereafter be used to call out to her, or take her hand if she's nearby.

So much of the charm and narrative innovations of *Ico* are framed by your relationship with Yorda. She rarely walks anywhere on her own, but will always try to come to you when you call out. You'll often take her hand, dragging her around as if she's vaguely lost and confused but with just enough confidence in you to not let go. In a subtle but affecting touch, you'll sometimes feel her footsteps through small vibrations in the controller— motors thrumming in protest if she's feeling especially reluctant—an effect used later in *Shadow* to bring you closer to your equine companion. Yorda doesn't hesitate the first time she has to jump a big gap to catch your hand, but takes a smart step back before she lunges and leaps. Similarly, while Ico hurries up and down ladders, Yorda places two hands and feet on each rung before stepping up or down, never tentative but ever careful. While the two children could have been made of different texture skins wrapped around the same character model and behavior set, significant attention was paid to make them feel like individuals.

Filling in the spaces between Ico and Yorda's often wordless communication is the ever-present wind. Even in the most interior chambers, a distant din of seaside air can be heard alongside your echoing footsteps or the crackling of fire, growing to a howling rush as you explore the far edges of its exterior. Many of the castle's spaces feel larger than they are as the wind expands through them and whips down passageways, and you even see it represented on Ico and Yorda's clothes, often blowing towards or away from exits and entrances. *Ico* isn't quiet throughout, though, as a sparse soundtrack accompanies many of the story beats and cutscenes, and even tiptoes into gameplay at times. Distant, distorted walls of sound haunt the darker moments, reverberating organs or synthesizers gone mad. Though *Ico*'s theme song—inspired by Simon and Garfunkel's "Scarborough Fair"—portrays the game more sunnily, a melange of Spanish guitar and wistful, vaguely Middle Eastern finger-picking, with an ebbing, soulful bass line.

· · · · · · · · · · · · · · · ·

While Yorda's companionship provides the heart of the experience, *Ico*'s body of adventure lies amidst a vast, interconnected castle teeming with environmental puzzles to solve and pathways to uncover. Waterways need to be drained, beams of light rerouted. Blocks are used as stepping-stones and then recast as weights for pressure plates. The visual vocabulary of *Ico*'s puzzles feels familiar after a couple decades of adventure games, but within *Ico*'s castle they're particularly cohesive. The design rarely feels nonsensical; the castle is a place of ritual, utilitarian against the sweeping beauty of its seaside surroundings. And while it often feels like a tangible place that could almost exist on Earth, Ueda didn't visit any real-life ruins during its conception—he had a vision of it in his head already, inspired in part by the architectural sensibilities of eighteenth century Italian visual artist Giovanni Battista Piranesi (likely for the labyrinthine wonder of his "Imaginary Prisons" series).

While traversing the castle you'll regularly encounter a variety of shadow creatures, which single-mindedly try to carry Yorda into seeping portals on the ground from which they spawn. The creatures become increasingly animalistic and even demonic as the game progresses— always hewn of black fog, a Lovecraftian darkness of something your mind can't entirely process. Fighting them can feel like a messy and desperate chore, one that some players argue is the game's only true blemish. I can't imagine the game without it, though—combat makes the castle feel more alien and dangerous, and lends an unpredictable pacing. It also grants the quieter stretches of the journey a welcome sense of relief, and carefully sets up Ico's role as Yorda's protector before their inevitable role reversal, in the most impactful scene of the game. After countless rooms of leading Yorda by the hand and pulling her up ledges to safety, a decisive gameplay moment comes in which Ico must leap for his life, putting all of his trust—and the player's trust—in being caught by Yorda. It's a beautifully designed scene, two halves of a bridge separating with nowhere else to go, the ultimate test of the wordless bond that the characters have developed. Ninja Theory co-founder Tameem Antoniades knows something about that bond, having developed his own story of escorting another character through a foreign world in 2007's fantastic *Enslaved*. "To make someone care about a character requires a great amount of respect for humanity and representing its facets truthfully and subtly. […] We put way too much emphasis on trying to find mechanical innovation in games rather than experiential ones. The fact that I fell in love with a ghostly set of pixels in a world that felt real to me was *Ico*'s innovation."

As one of *the* early mainstream games to bear the banner of "games as art," *Ico* feels every bit as affecting today as it did the first time. Though it's (thankfully) now less of an anomaly in an ever-growing crowd of games about the human condition and the people we connect with, given visibility by commercial hits like *Journey*, *Gone Home*, and *The Last of Us*. Developer Naughty Dog's Neil Druckmann, creative director and narrative architect of *The Last of Us*, cites *Ico* as a key influence and one of the games that got him into the industry in the first place: "[*Ico*] was fantastical but believable; all of its architecture had an internal logic to it," he told *CVG* in 2013. "But the main thing I loved about *Ico* was that relationship; that hand-holding mechanic that helps build a bond. It was the first time I realized you can create something meaningful through interaction, as opposed to just telling a story." Games are special and unique *because* of those interactions; taking Yorda's hand has an exceptional power, one that couldn't be replicated in a movie, or a book, or a song.

*Ico*, before most, and with a bold confidence, understood that. By simply trying to make something different, Team Ico planted a seed that would quietly help the medium to grow to new heights—even if it was never the intent. AI programmer Jinji Horagai says it best, "I truly appreciate the fact that after 10 years from its original release, there are still so many fans of *Ico*. But back then, those things didn't enter our mind. We were simply playing our own Rock 'n' Roll."

# SHADOW OF THE COLOSSUS

*SHADOW OF THE COLOSSUS* OPENS on the wings of a bird, flying high and free. A lone rider hugs a narrow cliffside ledge, urging his horse across a gap in their path. They journey together across stark plains, past serene forested ponds, through rocky passageways. A soaring, almost gothic introductory theme plays—a choir swells over strings, and the delicate, searching trill of a flute.

The rider and his mount reach a vast stone bridge, stretching out over cliffs and canyons into the distance, towering over the land around it in all directions save for the structure at the very end. The design of the bridge is striking, each long curved supporting beam leaning forward against the next, ageless and immovable. It also serves as a visual counterpoint to the notably absent bridge in *Ico*'s opening—one that would lie between the cliffs and the castle—setting up one of the first of many subtle connections between the two game's worlds.

They eventually reach the structure at the end (officially known as the Shrine of Worship), as circling birds chirp over the howling wind. A stone door slides open by some unseen force, the horse staging a brief protest before being coaxed inside just as the door slides closed behind them. The horse and her rider spiral their way down a huge cylindrical chamber, past a small pool at the bottom, and a series of sixteen different, vaguely beastly stone idols. It's suddenly clear that a bundle slung over the horse is no bundle at all, but the body of a lifeless girl. The rider—our protagonist, Wander, whose name (in apparent Team Ico style) we won't learn until the credits—carries her to a waiting stone altar, setting her down gingerly before dramatically pulling off the cloak she's wrapped in, letting the breeze take it. The girl, Mono, is pale, with flowing black hair and a long, lightly patterned white robe. Her ailment is unclear, but she rests still as death.

The scene cuts to what appears to be a memory from Wander's (recent?) past, in which we see a mask floating against a backdrop of smoke and hear the sound of crackling fire—perhaps a village elder speaking to Wander before he left. The voice speaks in a backwards, swirling tongue, subtitles translating:

> "That place…began from the resonance of intersecting points…They are memories replaced by ens and naught and etched into stone. Blood, young sprouts, sky—and the one with the ability to control beings created from light…In that

world, it is said that if one should wish it one can bring back the souls of the dead…

…But to trespass upon that land is strictly forbidden…"

Jumping back to Wander's present, shadow creatures emerge from the floor, immediately reminiscent of *Ico*'s ever-shifting foes. Unlike Ico, Wander simply needs to *unsheathe* his sword, which shimmers with a deep light, to dissolve the creatures into nothingness. Thunder crackles high above, and a voice speaks from somewhere in the rafters—an echoing, inhuman murmur, filling the shrine: "We are the one known as Dormin."

Wander explains his presence, in his own foreign tongue: "I was told that in this place at the end of the world—there exists a being who can control the souls of the dead." Wander explains that Mono has a cursed fate and was sacrificed (another familiar beat from *Ico*), and asks for Dormin to please return her soul. Dormin laughs, musing, "Souls that are lost cannot be reclaimed… Is that not the law of mortals? With that sword, however… It may not be impossible."

• • • • • • • • • • • • • • • •

In the period between having submitted *Ico* for production but before it released, Team Ico experienced some rare downtime. It was then that Ueda began drawing storyboards for a concept video that would become *Shadow*. Ueda told Kenji Kaido that it felt like all the games he played had big bosses that needed to be shot at to be defeated, and wondered why he couldn't just climb up and kill them with his weapon—so they decided to take matters into their own hands, and more deeply explore the role of game bosses.

*Shadow* was a trojan horse for subtler, more mature storytelling and emotionally challenging themes, marketed foremost as an epic, action-packed adventure. It almost never got the chance to do so internationally though, as its US release was initially kiboshed in a Sony greenlight meeting. "The gameplay was a big departure from *Ico*," remembers then-director of product development Allan Becker. "The perception was that the team had bitten off more than they can chew." Becker insisted that the game would be a masterpiece, though, and that Sony would look stupid if they didn't pick it up for a localized release. I asked Becker what stood out to him about the game so early on. "Even in its early state," he said, "*Shadow* had an air of reflective wistfulness—that intangible something. [...] It's one of those few titles that transcends its boundaries as a game and moves into a true emotional experience, perhaps even spiritual?" Interestingly, *Shadow*'s success wound up primarily as an American phenomenon, dwarfing international sales and also trumping *Ico*'s sales by a substantial margin.

*Shadow*'s premise is even more dire than that of *Ico*—a dead girl, an adventurer willing to do anything to bring her back, and an ancient, mysterious presence setting the stakes. The key elements aren't too dissimilar to those in *Ico*, but the adventure is all the more grand, and tonally more mature. And while *Ico* may be the more seminal game of the two—opening the eyes of countless developers and gamers to the efficacies of storytelling through gameplay—*Shadow* will forever be the more singular beast, building on those same design tenets on a wholly different scale, never to be repeated.

The desperation of Wander's quest has always resonated with me, and ever since *Shadow* I've found myself playing games more in character. Within most games, I try to act how the characters would act in a given situation. I'm not Nick playing as Wander, I'm simply Wander. Some of that comes with making judgment calls about a character to decide *how* they would react, but it's typically an unconscious decision. In the open-world Western *Red Dead Redemption*, I *was* John Marston, a rugged gunslinger just trying to get back to his family. I was vicious if provoked but fair when I could be. Once I found out that there was a button to doff your hat, I simply had to do so to everyone I met—it's the polite thing to do, really. And in perhaps a more telling example, *my* John Marston walked when in towns, instead of running everywhere to save time. There's no in-game reason or benefit to walking, the AI characters don't care, but it simply felt right to me, the unconscious side of my player agency further immersing the conscious side through my actions. In *Shadow*, it doesn't matter that I don't know the specifics of Wander's motivations—I just know that I *have* to revive Mono at any cost, and I play the game with that same desperation, a self-sacrificial chip on my shoulder.

Whether you play wholly in character as I do or tend to keep your entertainment at an emotional arm's length, *Shadow* will put your feet to the fire and make you think about your actions in a way that few games ever have—it isn't just a game about conquering giant beasts, it's a game about how you *feel* about conquering them.

• • • • • • • • • • • • • • • • •

Dormin explains to Wander that the beastly idols must be destroyed if Mono's soul is to be returned, and that the only way for a mortal to accomplish this is to seek out and defeat colossi which serve as incarnations of the idols. The voice ends with a dark foreshadowing: "But heed this, the price you pay may be heavy indeed."

It matters not to Wander.

"Very well," Dormin continues, as the camera pans out of the shrine, and across a great sweeping landscape. "Raise thy sword by the light… and head to the place where the sword's light gathers… There, thou shalt find the colossi thou art to defeat."

# RAISE THY SWORD
# BY THE LIGHT

THE OPENING CINEMATIC ENDS as the camera transitions into live gameplay, and I'm given control for the first time. Moving Wander around is a joy, both in execution and for the fact that there's no particular rush or threat as I prepare myself for this world and its as-yet unseen battles. The shrine is empty, save for Mono lying still, and my horse Agro, quietly exploring nearby while I come to grips with the controls. Wander's gait is more mature than Ico's, the earned confidence of an adventurer rather than that of a resilient child. His jumps are fearless lunges forward that can cover a lot of ground. If his sword is unsheathed, he'll run with it ninja-like, pointing it down and back along his side. And many of his basic movements are contextual—he'll leap from a running horse, or simply dismount with a step down from a stilled one. Agro is a star in her own right—a living, breathing companion and partner in crime for Wander, not simply a vehicle for speed or safety. And when I'm not riding her, she'll wander off on her own, or rein up dramatically alongside me without prompting, or stay close when staying close is called for. She's unpredictable, as animals are, but a fierce friend and really my only one in this world.

As we leave the confines of the shrine, the true breadth of this place—the Forbidden Lands, as they're known—becomes evident, and with it a mounting sense of adventure. It's breathtaking. Rolling wind-swept hills and crags flow off into the distance ahead of me, overcast skies above burning with sunlight just behind the clouds. The camera stays low, following behind and keeping Wander off-center, maintaining focus on the landscape. Even while casually exploring, there's a sense of cinematography to the framing, some distant director playing up the drama of each shot while maintaining a visual balance.

An old companion returns in the howling wind from *Ico*, making the Forbidden Lands feel just a bit more lonely and desolate. While I can charge off in any direction and explore for hours, I won't be able to progress without finding and defeating the first colossus. Dormin has given the first hint—"Raise thy sword by the light"—and holding the Circle button does just that, reflecting the sunlight off of my sword to create a simple 3D radar that focuses from a wide net down to a tight beam as I point towards the location of my next foe. This works on foot or while mounted, as long as I have access to sunlight (which adds a challenge in some shaded spots later on). It's an elegant replacement for a traditional waypoint marker that avoids the visual busyness of so many modern games.

The first colossus lies directly south, a relatively quick journey from the shrine straight across the plains to the cliff walls in the distance. Along the way, I pass a small oasis along the edge of a hill, a verdant outcropping surrounding a large tree. It's a bit unfair since I've played the game many times, but I know that the alluring fruit hanging from the highest branches can be retrieved with a single shot from my as-yet-unrevealed bow. I equip it with a quick flick of the D-pad, and hold down the Square button to nock an arrow and aim. The bow feels good, responsive, and once I've shot down a piece of fruit I can pick it up and consume it, slightly extending my health bar. This discovery may not happen during your first playthrough if you're not curious enough to stop or figure out the bow, but finding these fruits is one of the *very few* activities outside of fighting the colossi.

Back on track, l soon hit a shadowed basin below a cliff (roughly where the light directed me to), where a short cutscene kicks in. The camera tilts up to the top of the cliffs, as panpipes chirp a mysterious, searching little tune that tells me I'm in the right place. To scale the cliff, I'm given a crash course on how to climb mossy vines, roll under obstacles, pull myself up ledges, and jump from one handhold to another. It's a smart, concise introduction to the same tools I'll need to scale and fell my first foe (and subsequent others), if a bit overt with its messaging. Whereas *Ico* didn't put a single instruction on screen in its entire playtime, *Shadow* spells out all the basics up front through a short series of tutorial messages. It's certainly a more mechanically complex game than *Ico*, but it's a bit of a shame that the first few minutes lean more on non-diegetic instruction, when the atmosphere and storytelling are otherwise so immersive. This section also serves to separate me from Agro for the first time, which feels discomforting even in these early moments.

As I crest the top of the cliff, next to a thin cluster of trees, rocks, and bushes, from somewhere to my right comes an echoing bellow and a series of earth-shaking stomps. Massive, hoofed feet fill my vision as they tromp by, attached to legs like mossy oaks, and a huge armored hand swings low to the ground. The behemoth walks past me, trees rattling and a black cloud of dust kicking up in his wake, my controller rumbling with each monstrous step. I'm given back control of Wander before I've had time to fully process the scene, and all lonely comforts are forgotten. I focus on my new foe, birds circling above him as he patrols this canyon, wielding a massive club with gorilla arms. There's so much to take in—there have been no practice runs, no smaller enemies to cut my teeth on. I'm alone against massive odds. The creature feels like an ancient extension of this wild place, disturbed by my presence. The haunting colossus design has become an evocative touchstone of my mind's eye—this first colossus, the box art cover star who forever adorns my Mac's desktop background in a piece of fan art whose origins I've long forgotten. The colossus is terrifyingly top-heavy, a broad-shouldered brute with piercing blue eyes shining out from a face constructed of symmetric stone and a shaggy, shoulder-spanning mane of mossy fur. The colossi often look like long-abandoned temples come to life, elements of their bodies or armor seemingly designed by some great mason. "I avoided designs that made it obvious what the motive was," Ueda told *OPM* in 2005, "so I combined various things, like the front of a car or the surface of a building. Normally, things like that aren't used for monster design. By doing so, I thought that the colossi would have peculiarities, yet seem realistic at the same time."

Holding the L1 button will focus the camera on a colossus for as long as the button is held, immediately useful in taking in my foe while keeping my distance as I plot my attack. There's not much space in this clearing, and nowhere else to go—I could climb all the way back down, perhaps find some comfort in seeing Agro again, but there's no other way to progress. In this way, the game puts my back against the wall while at the same time placing the impetus on me to take action and make the first strike. The colossus patrols nearby, but Wander must disturb its path to begin the battle. While most traditional video game boss battles lock the player in a small arena with an enemy who immediately attacks, *Shadow* casts the player as the aggressor instead, a distinction with ever-growing importance throughout this tale. It's the beginning of many role reversals that become more evident as the game progresses—but like many things in *Shadow*, the theme starts more subtly.

• • • • • • • • • • • • • • • •

I wish that I could remember the feeling of playing out this battle for the first time, but it's just out of reach. My first hands-on exposure to *Shadow* was in 2005 on the blaring show floor of E3, the annual industry showroom hullabaloo. I was there to cover it for an enthusiast gaming blog (G-Pinions.com) that I ran with my friend Tom Mc Shea, and my primary takeaway was that E3 was simply the worst environment in which to experience something so nuanced, especially considering how excited I was for the game. Months later, Tom and I would crack open a final copy of *Shadow* in the more appropriate quiet of my apartment, and truly experience what it had to offer.

During that same period, I worked as an assistant manager under my friend Greg at an EB Games store in Chicago, where we took immense pride in championing all sorts of weird and unique games to our customers— through our infectious excitement, our store garnered the most pre-orders of *Shadow* in our district. Despite the hellish stereotype of working at a video game store, EB felt like the front lines of the gaming industry. Later, while reviewing games professionally, I would put a piece of criticism or a recommendation out into the world, and eventually it would garner comments, maybe influence a few purchasing decisions... but in those years behind the counter, people would ask me to recommend a new game, and I could walk them over to *Shadow*, bursting with superlatives, and place a copy in their hand. The best feeling in the world would come about a week later when they'd come in raving about it and ask me for my next recommendation.

While I was doing my best to champion *Shadow* online and in my store, other fans were taking further initiative—to bestow names upon the colossi, for which no official names are ever given (in-game or anywhere else). It's not entirely clear where these names originated—many cite a 2004 thread on the PlayStation forums in which user Thantanos mentions a "friend in Japan" who read them in an issue of *Dengeki PlayStation Magazine*, but by all accounts it appears that said issue never existed. Nevertheless, the intel apparently provided by this legendary Japanese friend has granted the colossi the closest thing to official names that they have. Complicating things further, Greg Off of Off-Base Productions—who wrote the original strategy guide for *Shadow*—explained to me that in the development build that he played while writing the guide, the game referred to the colossi by a different set of names (since forgotten), which he was later asked to remove from the final guide. It's likely that those were similar to what the development team referred to them by during production—in the case of the first colossus, "the Minotaur." I find his fan-bestowed name—Valus—much more personable, so let's stick with that. I'm also going to go with "him" for my colossus pronoun of choice, as the more anthropomorphic creatures read as male, and "him" feels more reverent than "it."

The battle begins by noticing Valus's furry achilles (a well-known weak spot, mythologically), which I can grab onto once I've evaded his earth-rattling stomps. Climbing a bit higher and unsheathing my sword, a glowing bluish-white sigil appears beneath the creature's fur. By holding the Square button, I charge up a one-handed stab of my sword while clinging on to Valus's ankle with the other hand, and letting go at just the right moment drives the weapon deep into Valus's flesh. He kneels briefly in pain from the impact, giving me a moment and a handhold within reach to scurry up onto the balcony-like structure built into his back. This also triggers a change in music, an appropriately epic blast of horns and pounding drums that mounts in intensity as I climb higher. The music throughout *Shadow* feels as if it's being orchestrated live, mirroring the drama, curiosity, or anguish of each moment.

I climb high enough to be able to run the rest of the way up his back and onto his broad neck, though stumbling and tumbling over in an attempt to stay upright while he shakes in protest and rears his massive head. It's at this point that players will realize that despite the relative precision of the jumping and grabbing—all the while discovering which parts of a colossus can be gripped—that *Shadow* is very much a game about trying to perform those actions under extreme duress, as if someone was slapping at the controller while you try to hang on for dear life. *Shadow*'s mechanical use of that verb—holding on—is also one of its most effective analogs for the real-life experience of playing the game. Bennett Foddy, an assistant professor of game design at NYU and the creator of the 2008 ragdoll runner *QWOP*, spoke to me about this link. "Generally in video games there is a very weak correspondence between the type of action you perform in the real world, on your controller, and the action that subsequently occurs in the game world. In *Super Mario Bros.* and every game that followed it, I press a button down and that makes my character jump into the air, even though compressing the spring under a button is not really anything like jumping into the air." Foddy notes that the gripping actions taken in *Shadow*, however, directly translate to how the player is manipulating the controller. As the player holds down the grip button for longer periods of time, it directly corresponds to Wander's fatigue, measured on-screen, even aching after longer sessions. "I feel more embodied in the character of Wander than I do in almost any other third-person game. It might be the best and deepest use of correspondence between controls and character actions that we've ever seen in a game."

Another central mechanical element that coheres the challenge, the colossi, the controls—and really the entirety of the gameplay—is the concept and measurement of Wander's stamina. As I grip and hold onto anything in the game—or hold my bow drawn, or swim underwater, or charge up a sword strike—a pink circle appears in the lower-right corner of the screen, and decreases as I continue the action. If I let go and return to a default state, the bar will slowly refill—in short, I can't hold on to anything for too long. This introduces a constant stream of strategic considerations when ascending and hanging onto foes, a lesson Valus teaches early on. Even once I've managed to get up to his back, I must seize the moment before I'm knocked off entirely. I need to get to the top of his head, and every so often it becomes necessary to let go of his fur and regain my grip while balancing awkwardly, like surfing a subway train without a handhold. I get my feet under me long enough to forge forward onto his head, where I find another glowing sigil. Valus roars desperately as I drive Wander's sword into this vulnerable spot, each time producing a thick arterial spray of inky black blood or some arcane lifeforce. His previously still blue eyes flash orange with… anger? Confusion? Fear?

Valus has a health bar of his own at the top of the screen, and the moment my final stab empties it a cutscene kicks in. Valus collapses bodily, falling forward limp upon the ground, a destructive collision of one big dead stone into another. At the same time, a mournful tune swells, a choir paying their respects to this difficult moment. This is no celebratory music, no triumphant Final Fantasy post-battle fanfare (a Pavlovian reward for victory in that series). There's no winning message, no experience points tallied, no positive reinforcement or typical game-like closure of any kind. The only indication that it's over is that Wander is still alive and the colossus is not. The music fades to careful strings as control is given back to me, while Valus's body is enveloped by black fog. Blue-black tendrils shoot out from the fog, hovering momentarily like undecided cobras before piercing Wander's body with their full force, a violent crunch juxtaposed with the serenity of the music. No matter how far I run in that moment, they always find me, an inescapable, futile dance. Wander collapses, his own body taking on some of the blackness, and the scene fades to white—and then into imagery of moving through a dark tunnel towards a bright light, swirling voices (maybe Mono's?) echoing from somewhere in the ether.

Valus is Ueda's favorite colossus, a critically important introduction to the true meat of the game— one that took significant trial-and-error to get just right. It feels unfair until the moment it doesn't, all the accomplishment of fighting a "boss" without the typical buildup. But at the same time I feel a bit conflicted by the violence of my actions and the reward of a solemn, uncelebrated death. It's clear even in this first victory that what I'm doing is wrong on some level, though I've journeyed too far to not continue at least a bit further down this road, into the depths of Dormin's deal.

After being given the option to save my progress, I'm taken back to the shrine. A shadowy figure stands silently over Wander's body, watching. How did I get back here? Was this wraith involved? Wander wakes, groggily, and the figure is gone. He immediately moves to check on Mono, who lies still as ever, though undisturbed. Somewhere, an organ swells, as one of the beastly statues nearby glows from within, a turquoise light piercing its cracks, before the whole thing shatters into rubble.

# IN THE SEASIDE CAVE

I'M GIVEN CONTROL OF WANDER AGAIN, who stands sternly facing the camera, Mono lying still as the sun pours in behind them, blurring the edges of the rocky tableau that lies just outside the shrine. Dormin has given a vague hint for the next colossus:

> "Thy next foe is…
> In the seaside cave…
> It moves slowly…
> Raise thy courage to defeat it."

Agro paces quietly nearby. It's comforting to see her again.

Before heading out, I travel deeper into the shrine instead, retracing Wander's steps back to the cylindrical room of the opening cutscene, running all the way back up the spiral ramp to the very top. It's real, walkable architecture in the game world—very little in *Shadow* is purely set dressing, or built for just one purpose and then thrown away. Touches like these help the Forbidden Lands to feel more like an actual place that can be deeply explored, should your curiosity take you there—you're limited only by the towering cliffs and perilous drops that border the edges of the world. A closed door awaits me at the top of the spiral ramp, perhaps unsurprisingly, but it's worth the quick side trip just to see (as side trips in *Shadow* tend to be).

I pay Mono another visit on the way out, peaceful in death as the wind catches the edge of her robe, a stir of false life rippling over her. I like the ambiguity of Wander and Mono's relationship. Are they friends? Lovers? Siblings? Is her condition something that he's responsible for? Is she simply a fallen princess and he an errant knight coming to her aid? Though his mission seems more desperate than that, risking everything in the hopes of reviving her.

Mono's altar is comprised not only of the pedestal on which she lies, but of a tall, shapely column of stone that extends down from the ceiling before flattening out to rest a few feet above her. It's wisely designed, not only for the visual gravity it lends that part of the shrine, drawing all eyes to the altar, but also serving as an obstacle for more curious players who might seek to climb on top of Mono's resting place. There's an interesting impulse in some players to break the intended immersion and instead be playful in serious spaces (like driving the wrong way around the track in a racing game); I tend to fight off the desire in the spirit of staying in character, but I have friends who'll jump at the opportunity to bring about chaos or narrative friction (looking at you, *Brendan*). The world design of *Shadow* tends to minimize those opportunities, stopping players from desecrating Mono's alter, riding Agro off cliffs to her death, or otherwise creating dissonance in the experience.

As I venture back down and leave ahorse, I'm struck by how gracefully the camera sweeps out of the shrine and across the plains to follow me. Wander isn't always the visual center of attention, and often appears small as the camera pulls out to frame the breadth of the landscape instead—Team Ico are much more interested in creating a sense of place than a sense of empowerment. In chatting about *Shadow* with Adam Saltsman, creator of *Canabalt* and director at Finji, he named the camera as his favorite thing about the game. Saltsman tells me about what he calls the "uncanny valley for camera work," a term he ascribes to the disconnect felt in most modern third-person action games between the cinematic presentation of the cutscenes and the invisible rig that players are dropped into behind their character when transitioning into gameplay. "Leaping between the two is massively jarring... *this never happens in Shadow*. I feel like nobody understands how insane this is, because it is entirely unique to that game. Nobody else has figured out how to do this. *Ico* does it but *Colossus* does it out in the wild. And at scale. It's just incredible."

*Shadow*'s seamless camera transitions are accomplished through a variety of methods, such as drawing the player's eye to environmental details that transform into gameplay objects, and using a different aspect ratio during cutscenes for cinematic impact before gently fading back to a gameplay perspective to keep it smooth. But primarily, *Shadow*'s harmoniousness is due to eschewing a static gameplay camera entirely. Rather than following Wander from a consistent vantage point or cutting between multiple ones (as in *Ico*), *Shadow* finds a rare middle ground—always keeping Wander in view, but carefully framing both story and gameplay moments with equal importance. That same invisible camera rig that sits behind most game characters is instead a free-floating directorial eye in *Shadow*, always considerate of the context of Wander's surroundings and his actions, be it in a long shot of riding Agro over an endless desert or in an uncomfortable close-up of the killing blow on a colossus.

● ● ● ● ● ● ● ● ● ● ● ● ● ●

Traveling across the plains once more, it's difficult to miss the beam of light now emanating from where I felled the first colossus, a spotlight piercing the sky and swirling the clouds above it. These beams will grow in number as I conquer more opponents, serving as visual landmarks to help me orient myself, but this first time it also serves as a reminder that despite the dream-like trappings of my battle's resolution and my mysterious journey back to the shrine, the fight was very much real.

I follow the light of Wander's sword to the next colossus, curving around and behind the shrine, further reinforcing the massive scale of the game and making sure I'm aware that my starting point is surrounded by explorable land on all sides, not just across the southern horizon. The light takes me across a natural stone bridge that spans a wide canyon, and down a long cliffside slope that ends in the shady shores of a beach, adjacent to a misty, enclosed lake. I can feel the coolness of this place, a nice contrast to the sunnier expanses above. One of my favorite touches here is the visibility of the very bottom of a few of the supporting beams of the bridge from the game's opening, huge columns embedded deep into the base of the canyon. Again *Shadow*'s architecture helps to tie its world together, naturally stitching new locations to previous visual landmarks.

I explore the beach for a bit, even wading out into the water, before checking the light of Wander's sword again, which points to a huge walled-off cave nearby. A familiar mysterious tune plays, letting me know that I'm in the right place. As I venture even closer, a cutscene kicks in as my enemy bursts through the wall and out of the cave—Quadratus (nicknamed the Mammoth in development), a giant four-legged bull-like colossus. The music changes to a more frantic clip, racing towards a resolution of its own. Quadratus walks on massive hoofed feet, peering down at me from between sharp curled horns (one broken off near its base), the bottom of its chin jutting out in stony columns like the front of a snowplow. His construction highlights a more distinct meeting of stone and moss, looking more like armor or an exoskeleton than rocky flesh. His back and the tops of his legs have plenty of stony architecture that might be able to be gripped, but his lower legs that stomp around me are layered in a smoother stone, so the path to my ascent isn't immediately clear.

As one of the least abstracted colossus designs— and a star of much of *Shadow*'s marketing materials— Quadratus is a regular recipient of fan art homages. There's a monument to him recreated block-by-block in *Minecraft*, an impressive papier-mâché replica covered in what looks like real moss complete with eyes that actually light up, and countless entries in a lengthy DeviantArt thread highlighting arts and crafts projects inspired by *Shadow*. As much as I've loved and thought about the game for over a decade, I haven't taken a deep dive into its fan culture until now. Much of it is simply a love letter to the game's memorable colossus design; even stripped of all context and placed on a table or a blank canvas, the designs are still wonderfully evocative.

• • • • • • • • • • • • • • •

This fight feels immediately different from the first as you never need leave Agro behind, and are likely still riding her as it begins. Ride close enough and Quadratus will rear up, exposing sigils on the bottoms of his hooves before stomping down menacingly. If you can loose an arrow at a sigil before that happens, Quadratus will cry out (sounding almost like an elephant) before kneeling down in pain on the corresponding leg. From there you must leave Agro once more, shimmying up Quadratus's mossy bits and up onto his back. It's a different world up there, much more steady but divided by a massive stone backbone of sorts that runs the length of the creature's body.

All told, Quadratus is one of the easier colossi once you've found your way up—simply destroy the sigils at the base of his backbone and on his head—but serves an important early lesson in familiarizing players with the more animalistic colossi. I remember having a tough time spotting the sigils on his feet and finding a way up the first time, which only adds to the appeal of replaying *Shadow*—problems that once felt overwhelming are often simple to execute once you've solved them. Despite all of the moving pieces, *Shadow* is a puzzle game foremost and an action game second.

Quadratus's beachside battle is reminiscent of a spiritually similar one in a much more mainstream game—that of the Scarab fight in *Halo 3*, an epic action setpiece that pits players against a giant walking robot. *Halo 3* game design lead Jaime Griesemer tells me that the battle was directly inspired by *Shadow*. The design team at Bungie was playing *Shadow* together over lunch when they had an epiphany about how much fun it would be to take on a giant, reactive creature with the Halo tool set. "Having something that big that would notice you and look at you and chase you and that you had to use your tools to figure out how to take down—it was just such a powerful idea. [...] *Shadow* really gave us the template for how to make that work. And so it was easier to sell it to people. [...] The psychological barrier was gone." Griesemer isn't shy about the inspiration—he's mostly just surprised that press never picked up on the similarities. "What's the quote, that great artists steal? To me the similarities are just so obvious, but maybe it's just because I saw it evolve. [...] I think a lot of people don't see past the context and the fictional overlay to the mechanics underneath—and so giant stone colossus and big metal scarab were very different. But really, mechanically, it's theft."

• • • • • • • • • • • • • • •

Upon my final thrust into the sigil on his head, Quadratus keels over, crashing into the sand as the music swells mournfully once more. Again I try to run from the black-blue tendrils that envelop him, and again it's in vain. They find me, and I'm whisked away to the tunnel of light, and then Wander is back in the shrine unconscious with two shadowy figures standing over him. Quadratus's statue bursts and crumbles as Wander awakens, ready for Dormin's next set of instructions.

Where Valus brought me across the southern plains and up a cliff, Quadratus took me across the northern land bridge and down into a canyon, giving a sense of the verticality and environmental breadth I'll be exploring in this world. I've already used both my sword and my bow, taken on a colossus alone and with Agro, and fought both bipedal and quadrupedal opponents. If Valus had been a carefully crafted introduction to the colossus battles, Quadratus was the first test to see if I'm paying attention. The key elements are familiar—cripple the leg, scale the back, reach the head—but each is slightly more obscured, challenging my observational abilities and pushing my newfound skills just a bit further. I'm not quite ready for anything, but I'm getting there.

# A GIANT CANOPY SOARS TO THE HEAVENS

I REALLY TAKE IN WANDER for the first time when he awakes. He's young, a teenager maybe, but clearly an experienced adventurer. He may have been headstrong coming to this desperate land, but it's clear that he knows how to survive. A pretty boy with almost shoulder-length crimson hair held back with a blue headband, his appearance leans towards androgyny. Matching blue shinguards are tied on with straps above his sandals, looking almost Grecian. He wears a stitched tunic and lightly patterned green shorts, forearms wrapped tightly in white cloth or bandages, with what look like feathers hanging from his belt. Most notable is Wander's serape or poncho, the bottom portion of which is patterned identically to the one Ico wears—their most *ico*nic (jokes!) similarity. In Wander's idle state, one hand rests on the scabbard that hangs loose from his belt, his sword clearly comfortable in the other. While his bow cannot be seen until readied, he brings it forth in one smooth, fast movement as he nocks an arrow.

Since gaming protagonists moved to the realm of 3D and mostly evolved away from cartoony mascots, they've often been sortable into gritty archetypes like soldiers, space marines, and treasure hunters. This is especially true of games developed in the West, whereas Japanese-developed games tend to have more flair, character, and visual panache. While Team Ico's games are relatively muted, there's a timelessness to Wander's design—vaguely low fantasy, but also of our world, functional and not over-designed. His construction is especially important in a game where you need visual contrast with the larger-than-life colossi—Wander's relative plainness makes it much easier to project yourself onto him, whereas a more colorful hero may have offered escapism at the cost of empathy.

White doves—similar to those that flit around *Ico*'s castle in the mist—have started to amass near Mono's resting place. Like the shadowy figures that look over Wander before he awakes, there are now two instead of one, part of several elements in the game that increment with each colossus killed. Shadowy figures appear, doves collect, idols crumble, and light beams pierce the sky—it becomes hard not to notice the growing impact of your actions. Following one of those beams, I backtrack to the place where I felled Quadratus. I find his body, or what's become of it: a jagged, mossy pile of rocks, fused with the ground. It looks as if it could have been there for hundreds of years, but only I know that it wasn't.

• • • • • • • • • • • • •

Climbing out of the canyon, the next colossus seems to be further north, my sword's light pointing to a passageway between rocky walls in the distance. There's a curious clashing of biomes here, arid desert and lime green grass mere feet from each other—and a tree nearby... covered in fruit! I find it easy to get distracted in *Shadow*, despite always knowing roughly where to go and what to do next. A black lizard skitters around the tree and when I kill with an arrow, it drops its tail behind. Around a hill I find a small, perfect pond next to some saplings; I imagine bringing Mono there to relax when this is all over. I follow a breadcrumb trail of lizards, working my way around the lip of the canyon that housed Quadratus, before eventually getting back on track and heading into the passageway.

I weave my way through narrow walls of stone until they open up into a misty valley, a crater housing a giant lake that I emerge at the edge of. In the center of the lake a huge island-like structure rises up, a wide column of rock that appears to be flat on the top, too tall to see, with an even wider stone structure embedded on the top, almost like a natural helipad or a crash-landed alien ship. A long, narrow curved pathway breaks away from it and ramps down, dipping into the water at its end. It's a beautiful, serene place to explore, though my destination is clear. I leave Agro on the shore and start swimming towards the base of the narrow pathway, headed for the top of the structure. Wander moves less confidently in water, keeping proper breaststroke form with his right arm but doing more of a sweeping doggy paddle with his left. He can also dive below the surface, at which point the stamina bar measures his remaining breath. The water is placid with no immediate threat, yet there's a tinge of tension in swimming for the first time, not knowing what may lie beneath the surface in the darkened depths.

I emerge at the base of the pathway and make my way up to the top. There, a few tricky, seemingly arbitrary jumps between handholds are required to get over to the main platform, which for most will likely result in a few accidental plunges back into the water far below. These handholds are actually serving a purpose, though, testing your skill at jumping between two back-to-back ledges, a big help in the coming fight. It also serves a secondary purpose, which is to inform players that they won't take damage from a high fall into deep water.

I crest the top of the platform, revealed as a broad, flat circular arena, tilted slightly, one that houses what may be my favorite colossus of the bunch: Gaius, called the Knight during development. I recall Dormin's description:

"Thy next foe is…
A giant canopy soars to the heavens…
The anger of the sleeping giant shatters the earth…"


What appears to be a pile of rocks near the center of the arena begins to rumble, then sits up, then stands fully upright as a bipedal, absolutely *towering* colossus. Gaius is roughly human in shape and proportion, emphasized and contrasted by Wander's diminutive frame in the foreground, while also looking like an entire ancient city come to life. An armament of columns and curved ridges of stone jut out from his chest, neck, head, and arms, somewhere between eroded armor and decorative regalia, atop a thick layer of furry moss. He also carries a massive blunt sword in his right hand, itself seemingly as large as the entire previous colossus. The camera stays low as I'm given back control of Wander—I can see the shrine distantly in the background, under a bright sky mottled with clouds, dry plateaus stretching away from the crater in every direction—and Gaius starts stomping towards me.

This battle is what inspired the Western name of the game, which needed localization from the Japanese title, *Wanda to Kyozō* (essentially "Wanda [Wander] and Colossus"). The credit goes to *Shadow*'s original US producer, Kyle Shubel, who worked on SCEA's International Software Development team (who made sure that games from other regions were appropriate for an American release), and his marketing manager at the time, Mark Valledor. Shubel explained to me that Wander was too confusing ("is that a name, is that a person, is that a boy, is that a girl?"), and that it took some fighting with both the Japan side and the US marketing team (who were trying to come up with something "hip and trendy") to land on a new name. But the Gaius fight helped them nail it, as Kyle explained to me: "It was the shot with Gaius when you would be running along and you'd swing the camera the wrong way […] and all of a sudden you would literally see the shadow of that I-beam that he carries as a sword come crashing down, and the shadow would pass over you like a jet when you're near an airport and it would freak people out."

Despite having played *Shadow* several times before, I'm breathless and overwhelmed by the odds of this battle yet again, and I can't quite remember what to do. Whereas I could fight the previous colossi at my own pace, even leave them alone completely for a while, I'm now stuck in this relatively small arena with a massive, armed giant closing in on me. He also seems more aware and sentient than the others, perhaps appropriate given his more human form. The encounter feels like a duel, two knights squaring off as if nothing else existed around them. I let Gaius smash his sword near me—a leaning, full-bodied windup that rapidly closes the space between us—and when it lingers in the earth I sprint towards it, scurry up onto it, and suddenly I'm running full bore up the length of this tremendous weapon. This may well be the most iconic moment of the game, as evidenced by the endless fan art trying to communicate the scale, impact, and sheer awesomeness of this interaction. It perfectly captures the David versus Goliath milieu of the impossibly bigger and stronger opponent being foiled by unmatched smarts and nimble ingenuity, and it requires a moment of spontaneous bravery from the player to run across such a perilous surface.

Few games can be said to provide these true moments of awe. Another is *Journey* (2012) by thatgamecompany, in which players adventure across a stunning desert world while reflecting on life and companionship. I spoke to its creative director Jenova Chen about the awe that both games are chasing. "Awe is when you don't understand something, when you feel that the mystery is so big that in contrast you are so small, so insignificant, so that you have exposed yourself towards something divine. We have to make the player feel small and so a large landscape is very effective in making you feel that. And that's also how church works—most churches have such a high ceiling, that makes you feel small and makes you feel this moment you share with God."

The religious allusions in *Shadow* are not easily missed, from the church-like construction of the shrine to the disembodied voice in the ceiling that is Dormin—or spelled backwards, Nimrod. According to ancient religious texts, Nimrod (the great-grandson of Noah) led the people of Shinar in the construction of the Tower of Babel, meant to reach up into the heavens. Seeing this, God scattered the people of Shinar across the earth, confounding their speech and giving rise to a world of mutually foreign languages. This is but one of several interpretations of Dormin's name, but the scattering of entities across a land certainly has growing importance in *Shadow*'s tale.

• • • • • • • • • • • • •

I can only scale Gaius so far before the armor at his elbow blocks my path and he flings me back to the arena below. It takes me long enough without progress that Dormin's disembodied voice chimes in with a clue, pointing out that the colossus's armor is brittle. It's a bit creepy, really, and it's unclear at this point why Dormin is omnisciently guiding me. I take his hint, though, and stand on a small raised platform in the middle of the arena; the next time Gaius takes a swipe, his sword connects with the platform and the piece of armor that was blocking my ascent shatters off, granting him a slight vulnerability.

I scurry back up the sword, up and around his elbow, and leap across to his midsection where a sigil glows brightly from a distance under the light of my sword (oh, it can locate sigils too—multi-use sword!). A few charged stabs (under great duress of Gaius fervently trying to shake me off) and the sigil is gone, leaving me one final tricky journey to the top of his head. As I clamber up his shoulder, there's a moment when Gaius seems to have forgotten me, looking out over the beauty of the sprawling lands, still and unthreatened. It doesn't last long, though, and he turns his attention back to the nuisance.

These final moments of fighting Gaius are monumental—it feels like a fight to the death at the top of the world, a clear view for miles in every direction save for the writhing titan beneath me. It's also the first time that the scale of the game is truly communicated. Wander, as a relative ant, on the apex of a stories-tall giant, who's standing on an arena, on top of a towering column of rock, in a lake, in a crater. Somewhere far below, my speck of a horse runs back and forth nervously on the shore.

# IN THE LAND OF THE VAST GREEN FIELDS

LET'S TALK ABOUT HORSES.

First, our equine companion in arms, Agro. A video game horse like no other. If you let *Shadow* idle at the start screen, it will sometimes take you in-game to the last spot you saved, where Wander lies asleep and Agro explores the lands by herself, while the camera follows above like a bird. One of the more peaceful, quietly stirring songs keeps her company, an almost Italian or Spanish arrangement of acoustic guitars. It's a beautiful way to see the world more passively, as Agro gallops across plains and trots carefully past chasms, exploring the countryside until the next time you need her. Another thoughtful touch by *Shadow*'s creators to further immerse you in their world.

• • • • • • • • • • • •

And now, a brief history of relevant horses in modern gaming. *Red Dead Redemption* is an incredible Old West epic where the horses are a lot of fun, but you're so often swapping horses that you can never build an attachment to your mount. The Elder Scrolls series of first-person high-fantasy sandboxes uses horses mainly as a means of speeding up travel, and also led me to a hilarious discovery that if you sleep to change the time of day while mounted on your horse, you'll awaken standing next to its corpse. *Darksiders*, an under-appreciated action game in which you play as War, one of the four horsemen of the apocalypse, features your horse Ruin, a massive fire-trailing Clydesdale that—once unlocked—gallops up out of the ground whenever you desire. It's awesome. And most recently, there's *Metal Gear Solid V: The Phantom Pain*, in which your horse—D-Horse—can be deployed into the field via balloon drop-off at any time, provided you have the cash.

The list drops off pretty severely after that, save for gaming's most widely beloved horse: the Legend of Zelda series' Epona, named after the Gaulish goddess of horses. While I'm not the biggest fan of the 3D Zelda games where Epona made her mark, I spent enough time riding her to get a feel for her role in protagonist Link's world and the unchanging purpose that she serves. On his blog The Pretentious Gamer, Bryan Ma—previously a designer at 2K Games—outlines some of the differences between the two companions:

As characters, Link and Epona have a similar relationship [to Wander and Agro], but to very different effect. The game continually illustrates their relationship through cutscenes, but the gameplay doesn't reinforce the emotions that the narrative is meant to promote. Although expressed as a central character figure and is often supposed to tug at our heartstrings ("Look, she's hurt her foot!"), in the game Epona fills the sidekick role, the tool of the player. [...] She disappears and appears and there is little expression of realism in communicating that Epona acts like something approaching a real horse. [...] At the start of the game, Agro also seems to be simply a tool for the player, but the shared experiences of fighting the colossi and wandering the landscape bring the player and Agro together. Although you control Wander, gameplay is a shared experience, in a sense. Rather than being an accessory to the experience, Agro is a necessity; dashing in and out of a colossi's view, leaping onto Agro's back as an enormous foot crashes down where Wander would have been. The sheer repetition of these events has a constructive effect on this formation of a player-AI bond.

Since *Ico*, several high-profile games have involved an ever-present partner character, though *Shadow* is the only one I can think of with an ever-present horse. And to me, Agro never feels like anything less than a *real* partner—a character with a mind of her own, one who is always aware and considerate of my intent. It's tough to think of her purely as an AI driven by different commands and behaviors. (In my notes I wrote, "maybe she's controlled by a real horse with a game pad somewhere.")

And while I ride her—through treacherous passages, across sun-beaten deserts, and into battle against overwhelming odds—I never control her directly. Where most game horses aren't functionally different to manipulate than their riders—move the analog stick right, and the horse moves right—Agro is different, acquiescing to Wander's instructions while still being perceived as a fully independent entity. I simply guide her reins in the direction I'd like to go, shifting my weight and giving her a small spurring with a sandal, and we're off.

Another nice touch is how Agro responds to Wander from different distances. Whistle from far away (one of those high-pitched whistles involving fingers, which I've always wished I could do), and Agro will often rear up, immediately charging back over to me. From a medium distance, Wander will instead yell out Agro's name, pulling his shoulders back as he does so to *push* the name out, "Agro!" (If you've played the game before, I'm sure you can hear it in your mind now.) If Agro is close enough, Wander will simply speak her name at a conversational volume, simply reminding his companion that he's close by. During combat, it becomes a more desperate, strained yell, an urgent expression of *are you okay?* Agro's concern for Wander is evident as well, as she whinnies in alarm when he falls from the top of a colossus or a high ledge. The controller's vibrations further increase this bond—in a slow trot, it almost feels like a joint heartbeat, whereas running harder pulses the motors with accompanying momentum.

Even at face value, the imagery of Wander riding Agro across the expanses of the Forbidden Lands is striking, and has inspired a range of homages. One that has brought me particular joy is the lesser-known mobile title *A Ride Into the Mountains*, a fantastic little action-puzzle game by Sunhead Games out of Taiwan. It clearly draws inspiration from *Shadow*, with striking pixel art and a smooth running animation for its horse, which was accomplished by pixelating the frame-by-frame animation of Eadweard Muybridge's 1878 *The Horse in Motion* (which you've likely seen as one of the earliest examples of the motion picture). While researching art styles for the game, Sunhead came across Darwin Yamamoto's "Pixel of the Colossus" fan art (please Google it) and pinned it to the top of their work software so that they'd see it every day. Over time, it influenced the look and structure of the entire game—the influence of *Shadow*, even a step removed through fan art, helped their two-man studio find the soul of their aesthetic.

All this horsing around can only lead us to one place, of course: the next colossus, who lies across the eastern plains through a network of shadowed, twisting canyons. I dip through a cave near the end, emerging at the edge of a beautiful, verdant valley, greener than anywhere I've yet seen and draped in vines and a thick carpet of moss. It's also noticeably more quiet and serene, far from the howling winds of the plains, replaced by the sound of a breeze through rushes, or perhaps an unseen waterfall. While the coming battle itself will be familiar to me, there's a gap in my memory to the introduction of this place, and the journey there feels wonderfully new and mysterious.

In the center of the valley, a small meadow holds four small hills, symmetrically adjacent to one another as four corners of a square. The outward-facing side of each is flattened off, bisected by a stone wall with an opening to walk through. Each opening leads down a short flight of stairs, which interconnects underground between all four hills. Around a far corner of the valley lies my foe: Phaedra, called Kirin during development after a mythical unicorn-like creature from East Asian culture. Phaedra is the first colossus I've been able to clearly see from a short distance before it comes to life, resting sphinxlike, the clear protector of this meadow. I walk close enough, and Phaedra snaps awake, standing up on long, bony legs, rib cage jutting out below his chest, almost the skeleton of a horse. Where Gaius was furry and dense, Phaedra is cadaverous, feeling especially old and mystical. Flanking his mask-like face dangle two long columns of decorative stone, like tassels or fallen reins, maybe *payot* even. (That's the most Judaism you'll get out of this Jew in this whole book, so enjoy it.) Its music is softer, more tentative, and the threat is less immediate.

I start to back up as Phaedra lumbers towards me, but Agro isn't moving from her spot where we both stood moments ago, and I panic—while I know she can't actually be killed, my concern for her supersedes that knowledge. I run back in for Agro, and Phaedra is upon us as I mount up, so we weave our way quickly between his legs back out into the meadow. I ride Agro to a safer spot near the entrance, and dismount to be more nimble near my foe. I look at Agro, who's looking at Phaedra, almost an ancient blueprint of a horse. (I wonder if she's thinking that too, because I'm a crazy person.) I duck in and out of the grassy burrows as Phaedra slowly pursues me on talon-like legs that crack the earth, and I fire a volley of arrows to lure him in Wander's direction as I try and remember what to do next. My sword indicates a sigil on his head, but I can't see any way to climb up, save for a few ladder-like stone rungs at the base of his coccyx, still too high for me to reach. Eventually I catch his attention long enough to focus him on the mouth of one of the burrows, where I promptly run underground and pop out one of the other entrances. Phaedra is still transfixed on my disappearance and leans down low to get a closer look, and my opportunity has arrived. I bolt across the meadow between us, and grab onto the rungs that were out of reach while he was standing. I climb up his back along the ridge of a mossy mane, and he tries to buck me off, rearing up on his hind legs in protest.

I flash back to a bad horse-riding memory from childhood. The first horse I ever rode—on what was supposed to be a peaceful forest excursion—jumped over a stream, shook violently to dry off, and suddenly broke away from the group to gallop full-speed across a field. While I walked away intact, I've since found horses to be terrifying in person, unpredictable harbingers of broken bones that I am wholly not comfortable being mounted on top of.

Wander and I are still clinging for life as Phaedra settles back down to earth. A glowing crack at the nape of his neck beckons my sword, and a well-timed stab there makes Phaedra lower his head slightly. I can't see a sigil anywhere, so I take a death-defying leap from his back over the frictionless stony armor that rings his neck, aiming to land on the top on his furry head. I hang in the air a moment, feeling the resistance of gravity, wind, and the momentum of jumping between two moving objects, before slamming down successfully on my landing spot, a blue sigil glowing brightly between my feet. It isn't easy, but the jump feels incredible, a high mark in my playthrough thus far.

A few brief stabs and it's over. I don't even run from the tendrils this time, standing saddened on Phaedra's motionless body as they whisk me away through the darkness and back to the shrine in our bittersweet routine.

This time, Agro trots over gingerly to check on Mono as Wander stirs awake. Still no signs of life. Agro whinnies and stirs when Dormin speaks next, but she doesn't leave my side.

# ACROSS A MISTY LAKE

THE FIFTH COLOSSUS LIES EVEN further across the eastern plains, past a winding cliffside trail overlooking a wall of waterfalls supplying a large body of water at the bottom of a canyon, an intriguing island poking out of the middle. At the end of the trail a small man-made structure catches my attention, the first of its kind I've encountered in this playthrough. These are save shrines, a glowing stone embedded in one wall, radiating energy. Kneeling before it, I'm able to save my progress in the field, as it were, rather than at the home base of the Shrine of Worship. I climb to the top of the structure, maybe two stories tall, up multiple ledges that are tiered like a wedding cake. As I stand on the very top, the camera pulls back, showing me the sweeping breadth of the landscape before me. It's as if *Shadow* wants me to take a moment and enjoy my surroundings at every opportunity, a respite from my dire mission and a reminder of the stillness and beauty of this land.

• • • • • • • • • • •

My girlfriend Amber and I went to Japan in the fall of 2014, the first time for both of us. It was an amazing trip, our first in a country where English isn't the primary language, a glimpse into the culture and customs of somewhere both ancient and ultra-modern. Kyoto was particularly memorable, a place we still reminisce about on a daily basis, and whose souvenirs now dot our apartment back in San Francisco (just as bits of our hearts will now always reside in Kyoto). I loved the pace of life in Kyoto, the juxtaposition of impossibly delicious restaurants blocks away from stunning ageless temples, and the feeling that everything was right in its place. Above all else, I would describe Japan's defining characteristic as *considerate*, at least as an outsider. Everyone was immensely kind, regardless of social stature, and even the most mundane aspects of life were thoughtfully envisioned and executed—in the budget hotel that we stayed for a couple of nights, the center of the bathroom mirror would stay heated during a shower as to never fog up. That small-yet-thoughtful innovation is Japan in a nutshell.

Being there also gave me context for the artistic motivations and inspirations behind some of the Japanese art and entertainment that I've enjoyed for years, from *Princess Mononoke* and *Seven Samurai* to *Katamari Damacy* and myriad Final Fantasies. Within much of Japanese art, there's a respect for the patience and curiosity of its patrons, and an aesthetic defined by ideals of imperfection and impermanence (*wabi-sabi*), subtlety (*shibusa*), and mystery (*yūgen*). The perfect words to describe *Shadow*, I'd say.

. . . . . . . . . . . .

My peaceful moment looking out from the save shrine is interrupted by a lizard tiptoeing just below me, this time with a white streak of a tail, skunk-like. I hop down and loose an arrow, and the glowing white tail is left behind as my prize, extending my stamina bar slightly. (I'll come to learn that one of these special white-tailed lizards can be found at each save shrine.) I head to a nearby tree that I spotted from up top, which droops with fruit that I immediately harvest the entirety of. I'm struck by the feeling that I'm decimating this place in more ways than one, but surely the fruit will grow back? This is the guilt that I'm now carrying, and it reminds me to get back on track with my greater (and ever guiltier) mission.

Through another stretch of canyon I find more antediluvian ruins, across from a rocky shore and rimmed with a sharp-looking wrought iron fence. It feels like the bowels of *Ico*'s castle here. I leave Agro on the shore and swim through an archway, climbing up a column of stone on the other side. A fenced walkway takes me to an overlook of what appears to be a sunken city, the peaks of its buildings poking out from the water. It's at this moment that the next colossus introduces itself, swooping majestically overhead before landing to perch on one of the tallest structures.

This is Avion, simply called the Bird during development, a magnificent colossus with broad spiky-edged wings, and an even longer tail—easily double its wingspan—that dips almost all the way down to the water from its perch high above. (According to Ueda, in the original design of this encounter the player would need to climb up its tail from underwater, which is why it's so long.) Avion is beautifully symmetrical, and one of the more literal recreations of a real-life creature in *Shadow*—beak, talons, and all. I'm also struck by the realization that I'm looking at Avion through the bars of a cage I've found myself in, as the overlook is surrounded by tall metal fences, completing the bird allusion.

Jumping down from the overlook through a hole in the floor, I swim to the structures jutting out of the water, pulling myself up on a low platform. Avion sits still, a sentinel waiting for my inevitable provocation. I fulfill my role of aggressor as I fire an arrow across the lake and into the body of my foe. In one sleek, silent motion, Avion rises from his spot, and in a single beat of his massive wings he's bearing down on Wander, flying low and alarmingly fast over the water. Before I have time to think, he's closed the gap entirely, and I'm jumping towards him in a desperate bid to land and catch a mossy strip on his wing. I brace for impact—even closing my eyes for a moment—and the next second I'm clinging to Avion as he whisks us away, higher and higher into the air, the water a distant blue backdrop below.

• • • • • • • • • • •

While *Shadow* is in part a product of Japanese culture, its design owes even more to the vision of Ueda himself. "Artist is the best term [for him]," Kyle Shubel (*Shadow*'s US producer) tells me about Ueda. "He can articulate his vision through words and through drawings. A lot of times he won't even tell you, he'll pull a pencil out and start sketching, and magical things happen. I hate to mystify the man further but he's incredibly creative, he's in his own world, and he knows the goal that he wants everyone around him to achieve well before he communicates it to them." The more you read and hear about Ueda, the easier it is to understand why *Shadow* is so extraordinary. According to Shubel, Ueda isn't even much of a gamer himself, finding most games to be too much of a diversion and choosing instead to spend his time working on his art and his writing. Even so, he managed to surround himself with like minds at Team Ico, a team that truly believed that they were doing something special and trusted Ueda to see them through it. "For being a quiet guy, Fumito is a very compelling man. He really inspired people… it was [like] being on the state champion football team—you all believe you're going to win your next game."

And like any champion team, they had to put in the hard work and overtime to see it through. Often Shubel would visit the studio to find producer Kenji Kaido asleep under his desk, his jacket hung from underneath his keyboard as a makeshift curtain after having been at the office for days on end. Kaido may be the unsung hero of Team Ico's legacy. Just as hearing more about Ueda clarifies *Shadow*'s vision, hearing more about Kaido clarifies how the team actually pulled it off. "You could see him watch Fumito go off on one of his tangents and his idea and you'll just watch Kenji start writing down notes. [...] Kaido is programming and production, Fumito is art and design—they are opposite sides of the same coin. Kenji was the one who reined Fumito in so that the games would ship eventually. [...] They compliment each other's weaknesses, they enhance each other's strengths."

• • • • • • • • • • • •

I'm in the thick of an airborne battle, completely removed from the quiet comforts of the watery ruins I enjoyed moments ago. While the other colossi encounters were thrilling, Avion is an absolute *rush*. A frenzy of strings rises and falls as a choir swells in time, underscoring the drama of the moment. The wind whips by as I alternately cling to and surf the length of this beast, as what look like orange embers fill the skies around me. Avion's movements feel reactive to my own, and he twists sideways as I sprint the length of his body, perpendicular to the ground as he soars. I'm forced to cling on tightly until he flattens out, and I run to the base of his tail, where I stab a sigil. After, I have no choice but to push my way back upstream, against the wind, the light of my sword revealing another sigil on the mossy tip of his wing. I nervously scurry across the slippery stone middle of the wing—the ultimate risk at this height—hoping that Avion stays level. Successful, I drive my sword into the glowing moss. Avion shrieks in pain, and twists *fully upside down*, so that I'm dangling completely off his body, gripping onto the moss for dear life. Kenji Kaido was once asked at what point during *Shadow*'s development did he feel that it was going to be a game that 'came from the heart': "For me, it would have to be when I lost the impression that the colossi were moving according to obvious AI algorithms. I felt it all of a sudden one day while I was testing the gameplay. The colossi didn't feel alive, and they didn't feel like animals, but they weren't machines, either. That felt right to me."

I'm running out of stamina, and I plummet down, down, with a splash into the water below (luckily missing the less-forgiving ruins poking up from it), and everything is quiet and peaceful again. I've come too far, though, and I need to finish the fight. Avion cruises tranquilly above, and I re-engage his attention with an arrow. He swoops down, I jump (to the other wing this time, thinking ahead), and we're back up in the skies together, stumbling and shrieking.

Avion is a resetting of expectations, and a favorite colossus for many of the developers I've been speaking to. I asked Ueda for his thoughts on why this battle in particular resonates so strongly. "I think this flying boss allows players to feel the weight and presence of their hero character in the game world," he said. "Players break away from the confines of the world's gravity and soar along with the boss, but only for a moment. If the game had many bird-type bosses, it would have made that sense of liberation from the ground less special."

I finish Avion off with a stab to his other wing, and his death knell takes over. I'm thrown from his body, as black blood sprays from his wing, an airliner out of balance and out of fuel. He crashes into the water, instantly submerged, sinking to the bottom of this flooded city. I try to hold my breath underwater to hide from the tendrils, dancing in the distance over Avion's resting place. It takes a few long beats, but they eventually separate from Avion completely, shooting out like symmetrical lasers before honing in on me.

# IT LUSTS FOR DESTRUCTION

SOUTHWEST OF THE SHRINE OF WORSHIP lies a cool, sun-dappled forest. Not too dense with trees, but with a thick enough canopy of leaves to let only bright rays of sunlight in. I quietly ride Agro through this still, peaceful place on our way to the next colossus, vaguely following the light of Wander's sword. It doesn't work in shadow, though, and we're left to our own devices to find the best route through. But first, I make sure to purposefully head the *wrong* way out, something that I've done for a lifetime in most every video game I could. That's usually how you find the best treasure and the most obscured secrets. It's a systematic dismissal of the correct next step, blowing off maps and navigational arrows to read between the lines of what the game *really* wants you to do: "Psst, don't go there, go *here*." Taking the wrong path first so often rewards us that it's become the only sensible thing to do; the way to see the most that a game has to offer, knowing that it will inevitably loop us back around to the correct path soon enough.

The off-the-beaten-path discoveries vary hugely between games, of course, but I like the idea that gameplay itself is simply a means to an end, to indulge human curiosity and a lifelong quest to become closer to the unknown. *Shadow*'s rewards aren't always as tangible as most, except for the slight health and stamina boosts that fruit and white-tailed lizards provide. But I often find myself exploring simply because it's beautiful.

My wrong route takes me to a treacherously narrow path along a cliff, leading to a dead end where a fruit tree hangs over a long drop to a reservoir below. I'm struck with a mixture of nostalgia and déjà vu. There's a white-tailed lizard here to grab, a rare sight away from the save shrines, but the branch holding the fruit is growing out over the drop, so my usual routine of shooting the fruit down and collecting it off of the ground won't work. It's a stymying scene that's stuck with me for years—this isolated tree growing at a dead end, with forbidden fruit that I can't gather. It feels both natural and specifically authored, hand-placed by a level designer with a playful smirk on their face. "When you're constructing a world, it's boring if everything is just there for logical or functional reasons," Ueda tells me. "We left in some noise on purpose."

I weave my way back through the woods, connecting with a new trail that leads me through a variety of biomes before spitting me out into a wide, arid desert. The light off the sword points me all the way across the sand, to the symmetric face of a temple embedded in a broad, imposing cliff. I find a sly entrance at its base, and leaving Agro behind I venture into a series of underground tunnels, taking me deeper into the bowels of the mountain. Eventually I emerge near the top of a massive, subterranean hall. Scaling down nearby ledges to the floor below, no sooner do Wander's feet touch the ground than a huge adjacent wall lowers, revealing the sixth colossus, Barba.

According to Ueda, Barba (called Minotaur B in development) is a sibling of Valus, the first colossus, another one of three Minotaur-esque creatures. He looks similar, though perhaps more well-preserved in this lair, his many outcroppings of armor fully intact, his limbs even thicker and more muscled. He wears a different mask, too, and diminutive horns jut out of his head on both sides. He's also aggressive, needing no provocation, and immediately heads towards Wander, smashing and stomping the ground nearby. I make a break for it across the huge hall, running full-speed towards a low wall, scurrying up and over it moments before Barba comes crashing through. This is a true pursuit, an angry giant after a panicked flea, and we scurry and crash through two more low walls before I reach the protective confines of some ruins at the end of the hall.

I hide behind a pillar as Barba stomps around, eventually leaning down to look for me more closely. This reveals Barba's defining physical characteristic, and biggest distinction from Valus: a long, layered beard that hangs in front of the ample mane that covers his chest and shoulders, and now hangs freely in front of me, beckoning.

I have a complicated relationship with beards. Which might sound weird coming from a guy who's very much known for and defined by his beard, both personally and professionally. I couldn't grow any whisper of a beard until my early twenties, at which point I made up for lost time, and within a few years I was more often fully bearded than not. I've only been clean-shaven twice since I moved to California almost nine years ago, and my beard is now inseparable from my identity. I get very kind, very regular compliments from strangers of "nice beard!" And while I thank them, I also think, "I basically did nothing for a while and now it's here." And while I've come to terms with the fact that I have a pretty good beard, I don't like being defined by my beard, the way certain colleagues feel the need to comment on it *every* time they see me, as if we have no other way of connecting. Still, having a beard feels sort of primal and even masculine—a characteristic that doesn't come easily to someone who can't throw a football properly and thinks his car runs via magic. As a result, I often *do* define myself by my beard (as I did in the introduction to this book). Like I said, it's complicated.

So with apologies to Barba—I mean come on, his name is basically "Barber"—I remember him primarily as the bearded colossus. And when he presents the opportunity, I take a running leap forward to grab on. I'm successful, and as he stands back up I leap horizontally, working my way up and around his beard to his mane, and up onto his back. There's a sigil on his head that I take out with a few desperate stabs as he thrashes beneath me, almost fully draining my stamina several times as I try to hang on. He eventually succeeds, and I run around on the ground for a while, trying to spot the second sigil with the light of my sword while avoiding Barba's stomps, until I narrow it down to his back. I hide for a bit, shimmy back up the curious beard, and work my way over to a familiar glow on his left shoulder blade. It's a tough spot to cling to, but I get in a couple of stabs and it's over. Barba crashes violently forward as the orchestra plays him off.

In the grand scheme of *Shadow*, Barba is one of the least interesting colossi, especially coming on the heels of the thrilling airborne battle with Avion. But he's also a smart step in pacing and contrast, and serves as a pop quiz to test out some of the techniques learned from previous battles. According to Ueda, "Humanoid colossi have some pliability and can move in a variety of ways, so it was easy to come up with ideas for this one." This may have been a case where one of the first ideas was solid (climb the beard!), and the implementation gave them a colossus flexible enough to slot into the lineup where needed, even if it wasn't one of the stronger ideas on its own.

My girlfriend had been watching this fight from the sidelines, but she missed the ending, so when she returns

I excitedly tell her where the final sigil was located. On Barba's *left shoulder blade*, in the exact same spot that *I've* been having sharp recurring pain for the last couple of years. Amused, I summarize the similarities between us—lengthy beard, weak spot in the shoulder blade, and I realize there's one more: it's a bright, beautiful Saturday outside, our blinds are drawn, and we're holed up in the darkness. Like it or not, Barba is my colossus today.

# A RIPPLE OF THUNDER

WANDER IS SINGLE-MINDED, seemingly numb to the tragedy and gravity of this murderous goose chase, but for me it hasn't gotten any easier. *Shadow*'s stakes are uncommon, to say the least—there's no world-threatening crisis looming, no immediate timeline on Mono's further deterioration. Nothing would come to further harm if Wander—or I—were to simply walk away. But Wander is defined by his persistence, enduring his quest in the hope that all this death will amount to a restoration of life, and I mean to see him through it.

Despite living in a light state of existential crisis most of the time, I don't have much of a relationship with death outside of art and media. My college roommate Adam died from overdosing on heroin not long after I'd moved out of a bad living situation with him. My grandfather Julian died of ailing health, across the world in New Zealand. My great uncle Lionel Abrahams died in my birthplace of South Africa in 2004, an amazing man described as "the yeast in the dough of South African literature" in his obituary in *The Independent*. Lastly, my childhood cat Kenja died in 2010 at the ripe old age of seventeen (or so), living with my dad in his cottage in upstate New York for the last few years of his life. That one hit me hardest by far, and it's still something I can't think about for too long without getting misty-eyed. All that is to say, maybe I'm impacted more by fictional deaths than most, since I gratefully have not been exposed to much real death in my life thus far.

I'm glad that *Shadow* is so reverent in its moments of death, something made to be so ubiquitous and casual in countless other video games. In a 2011 interview, Ueda discussed his first time infusing a colossus's death with melancholy:

> When we started developing the game there was no music composed yet, so for that scene when you beat him I added something provisionally, some sad music from a movie soundtrack. When I did that, all the staff who saw that scene burst out laughing. To have a scene like that, where you would expect some triumphant trumpet fanfare, but instead you hear sad music… it must have seemed like a mistake to them. I remember that experience very vividly. You know, deciding things by majority has its merits, but I think there's a danger that lies in that too. After we had officially released *Shadow of the Colossus*, I asked

players if they felt anything uncomfortable or awkward about that scene, and they said no.

It's a difficult thing to ask players to empathize with barely sentient beasts, especially ones that are often trying to kill you. But Ueda's clear authorial direction and that "rock 'n' roll" spirit that served the team through both *Ico* and *Shadow* make it work completely. I had experienced mature moments of storytelling in games before, even cinematic character deaths such as the infamous killing of Aeris in 1997's *Final Fantasy VII*. But games are defined by their interactivity—what you can *do* as the player, not what can be passively *told* or shown to you. It's something that I desperately wish film critic Roger Ebert would have understood before he died, being one of the more vocal critics of games as art—it's an impossible task to judge an artistic medium without experiencing what defines it firsthand. *Ico* was the first time that I had connected deeply with a story in gaming, told not only through minimalist plot points that respected and encouraged my curiosity and imagination (like many of the best films do), but told by *playing it* (like only games can do). *Shadow* resonated with me even more, and allowed me to feel loss, and guilt, and regret.

Games could be just as compelling when focusing on more ambiguous rewards than simply being fun—a small but formative revelation in the way I thought about the medium. Vander Caballero, CEO of Minority Media, understands this deeply. Caballero was creative director on *Papo & Yo*, a fantasy adventure told as a parable for his relationship with his alcoholic father. Caballero cites *Shadow* as providing the foundation upon which he built his story, inspired by the emotional conflict of defeating a colossus. But he first had to distance himself from years of design reflexes acquired during big-budget studio development. "One of the main points of [internal] disagreement was when people on the team made a fun level, for its own sake, but which didn't fulfill any emotional point in the narrative. I had to convince them that, even though it was a great level, we had to shelve it because it didn't deepen the game experience. Thinking about it in retrospect, it's kind of funny, because canning a level just because it's fun is one of the most counterintuitive things you can do in game development."

These days, the idea that games can be more than just fun is something I take as a given. And with the meteoric rise of independent games, the risk is much lower for a game to tackle something personal or profound, more interested in commenting on the human condition than shooting things (not to say that they're mutually exclusive, but sadly in gaming they usually are). *Shadow* was one of the first big-budget mainstream games to take these risks, helping in some small but important way to imbue countless games with more humanity and less cynicism.

• • • • • • • • • •

I'm exploring a stretch of rolling lime green hills, stopping to chase lizards. I'm lost, but it doesn't matter—the lizards' crafty AI is keeping me plenty busy. I climb to the top of each save shrine I see to take in the landscape and get a bird's eye view of where its accompanying lizard may be skittering below me, but it still takes another few minutes of cat-and-mouse with each before I pin it down with an arrow. For a time *I'm* the giant, hunting my tiny foes while they elude me in the ruins.

I'm still lost, driving Agro across blinding sands, between circular canyons, and through desolate ashen forests. I find that if I simply hold down the X button after tapping it twice, Agro will find her own way through tight turns, navigating even more smoothly than she would if having to guess my intentions. We finally find the hideaway of my seventh foe, past low ruined walls and across a long dilapidated bridge over water, not unlike Avion's lair. Again I must leave Agro, leaping to climb a tall lookout tower, from which I can see my foe resting just under the surface of the water below me—a long, snake-like form, buzzing with blue electricity.

Hydrus is something between an eel (as he was referred to during development) and a Chinese dragon, long whiskers and short fins trailing alongside his body. A beautiful shot from deep underwater shows his silhouetted form beneath the bright sky, a long, sinuous shape curving slowly in the water. He's likely the most obscured colossus, with an air of mystery all his own.

After I nervously paddle Wander nearby, Hydrus circles deep below before coming up to make a more deliberate pass at me. His head cruises past, followed by three orange protrusions, one at a time down the length of his body, each crackling the surface with electricity as it passes. Finally, his mossy tail splashes up for a moment before dipping under, wide like a whale's, allowing me to grab on the next time he comes by. When I do, he pulls me underwater without hesitation—the beginning of a peculiar battle in which we'll both be forced out of our element.

Lengths of Hydrus's body surface long enough for me to run down it in spurts, always stopping to cling on fiercely before he dips back underwater, pushing Wander's breathing capacity to its limits. His orange spines are useless above the water, but when submerged they light up with electricity, sapping large chunks of my life bar away if I'm nearby. Each spine has a failsafe, though—a small glowing "off" switch of sorts directly behind it that's disabled with a quick stab of my sword, turning it black and useless. I barely manage to take out the first two spines between running breaths when Hydrus has had enough and dives deep below, returning to his more peaceful state and leaving me desperately kicking up towards the surface. I almost drown twice this way, eventually luring Hydrus back up to the surface to finally disable the third spine.

There's a sad moment when Hydrus becomes especially hard to see underwater, and I realize that it's because I've rendered him fully powered down and harmless, and I want nothing more than to leave the fight. A beautiful water dragon, alone in a misty corner of the world, less of a threat than ever. Isn't this good enough? Why am I killing these hapless colossi when it makes me feel bad? Why am I even playing this dumb game?

I must finish what I've come for, though, and this time I make it up to his head before he can dive deeply, planting a few swift stabs as he tries to buck me off with his final movements. I want him to succeed, to dive deep and never come back up, but perhaps he needs to breathe as well. I hold tight, and my sword finds purchase a final time. Hydrus's body sinks, bending in a U-shape as his weight pulls him deep below, tendrils shooting up to find me at the surface. The music may tug at my heartstrings, but the deeper storytelling lies in my actions—someone is manipulating me here, and it's not clear whether it's Dormin, or Ueda. Or both.

# A SHADOW THAT
# CRAWLS ON THE WALLS

THE LOS ANGELES-BASED GAMING COLLECTIVE The Arcane Kids have a great line in their development manifesto that I think about often: "The purpose of gameplay is to hide secrets." It's a game design ideal to live by, and one that feels particularly apropos for *Shadow*'s deeply enigmatic milieu. Even at face value, *Shadow* is a game that drips with mystery, a result of stirring players imaginations with a refreshingly minimalist narrative that requires extrapolation, no baseline historical knowledge of anything in its world save for Wander's core motivation, and a very un-video-game-like embracing of empty space and unfinished ideas. The mood that the game creates is that of the uncharted; each colossus is a treasure to hunt, and a puzzle to unlock. Even their origins are obscured until the end of the game. But what true secrets is *Shadow*'s world still hiding? Beyond the intrinsic mystery of its aesthetic, is there anything left to be discovered?

A dedicated community of fans have been looking for almost a decade now, making exponential progress since 2009 thanks to the work of a few key people, led in recent years by Michael Lambert, a.k.a. Nomad. An Australian graphic designer by trade, Nomad has spent countless hours of his free time cataloging every corner of the Forbidden Lands, both through thorough exploration as anyone else could with enough time and skill, and through the aid of computer software that allows him to "hack" an emulated version of the game (as well as earlier unfinished versions), systematically combing through every nook, cranny, and line of code.

Nomad's discoveries are innumerable, all documented in excruciating detail both on his blog and through a series of accompanying YouTube videos (which have a mysterious quality all their own since Nomad never speaks). I've never seen a piece of media, or really anything I can think of, broken down as thoroughly as Nomad has done with *Shadow*. And with a game whose few overt answers only introduce more questions, no theory feels too crazy to pursue, and Nomad has backed several of them up with fascinating evidence. Some of my favorites include the idea that previous wanderers have been through the Forbidden Lands before (due to several of the colossus arenas having traces of previous battles), the many overlapping elements between *Ico* and *Shadow* (the relative timelines of their stories, the intriguing but unstated connections between their characters), and the now infamous Intersecting Points

Theory. Postulated on the Official PlayStation Forums in 2007—in the same "Quest for the Last Big Secret" thread that would later ignite Nomad's search—users pieced together what seemed like clues from the game's script with symbols found throughout the game world to yield a set of coordinates on the map which lay directly over the eleventh colossus's lair (coordinates seemingly also supported by laying the game disc's artwork over the in-game map). In the back of that lair lies a closed doorway, and if players could only find a way to open it it would yield something special… or so the theory went. It doesn't really matter what that something is, as *anything* likely would have sufficed for a community so deep down the rabbit hole together. As Nomad told Eurogamer in 2013, "It was the search that was the thing… I like to say it's like a Rorschach test, people imprint whatever hopes and beliefs they have onto the vast empty landscapes and see secrets that aren't there—they just hope they are." Nothing lies beyond the door, as user Radical Dreamer would later prove conclusively using game hacks, but it hasn't stopped the community from further theorizing about the intersecting points.

The other half of *Shadow*'s air of abstruseness lies in what was cut from the game. Ueda originally envisioned the experience with 48 colossi, but quickly realized that wasn't doable and cut it down to 24. Work then began on all 24, as they were modeled in 3D and ascribed different attacks and weaknesses. The team still had concerns about maintaining their quality within the timeframe of development, though, and instead settled on the sixteen that ended up in the final game. In doing so, elements of different colossi were combined along the way, making the remaining ones more interesting and also salvaging as much of their work as possible. While it may seem like a drastic reduction in scope, it fits right into Ueda's design sensibilities as he explains them: "I have the tendency to ask myself whether or not something makes sense and whether or not it's elegant in terms of game design. Like pruning tree branches, it's necessary to cut things out in order to improve the quality of a game."

With so few elements core to the experience of *Shadow* and such a breadth of beautiful colossus designs, it's no wonder that the eight cut colossi have been a topic of such fascination by both fans and the gaming press. And unlike most cutting room floor content, Team Ico has embraced their existence, with Ueda speaking openly about the specifics of their design. Several pages are dedicated to the lost colossi in the beautiful Japan-only official *Shadow* art book. All eight colossi were seemingly functional to some extent when cut, and although all we have is still imagery to appreciate them, it's a treat to see what could have been: a towering phoenix, a charging boar, a strange sandworm, a soaring roc, a spindly spider, a stalactite-swinging monkey, a creepy devil, and a noble griffin. Nomad has painstakingly researched where these colossi would have been found on the map, matching sparse environmental details found in early screenshots to similar bits of landscape that ended up in the final game, even comparing rogue textures left in the game code.

The art book shows sketches of even more creatures, like a gaunt sloth, a finned fish, a winged insect, and a gargantuan warthog. The final lineup of colossi has an impressive cohesion that I take for granted at this point, and while it's interesting to see a glimpse of what almost made it in, I'm not convinced that another year of development would have necessarily changed the colossus count. "The intention was to choose the sixteen best Colossi and focus on making those ones even better," Ueda told *Edge* in 2013. "I think we were halfway through production when we decided to reduce their number. Oh, there's certainly leftover test data and half-edited [areas], but it's a bit like the Minus World in *Super Mario Bros.*: I think it holds more romantic appeal if you don't know the specifics."

● ● ● ● ● ● ● ● ●

The location of the eighth colossus feels more concealed and exciting than most, and typifies much of the sense of mystery that lies at the heart of *Shadow*'s experience. It starts familiarly enough, through canyons and across fields… and then deep into an echoing cave, where Agro trots gingerly across narrow walkways of stone while the sounds of a nearby waterfall fill the caverns. Deeper still, the cave opens up widely, letting sunshine in from above and illuminating a stunning dilapidated temple at the center of a shallow lake. Swimming across the lake, I encounter a relative bounty of life: long carp-like fish, one of which takes me on a brief ride underwater when I swim close enough to grab on. It's a bittersweet moment coming so soon after Hydrus's death, but an undeniable treat, a rare burst of wildlife in an often desolate world. When I climb up on land, Agro splashes across the water to join me on a walking tour of the temple's exterior. It's one of those places that's hard to reconcile as something created by an artist, a perfectly organic balance of light, overgrowth, and crumbling architecture. It's one of my most treasured spots in the game. I must go deeper still, though, remembering Dormin's clue:

"Thy next foe is…
A tail trapped within a pail deep within the forest…
A shadow that crawls on the walls."

Forced to leave Agro behind again, I climb through the temple's sole doorway, heading down, down, deep beneath it, to a cylindrical chamber that holds my next foe. Kuromori lurks at the bottom of this chamber, the smallest colossus yet, but still a fairly large Komodo dragon-like lizard, called the Gecko during development. He reminds me of an anteater too, with a broad, flat tail—maybe a touch of skunk, or even pangolin, a beautiful armadillo-like creature found in Asia and Africa that's sadly endangered. Kuromori radiates with yellow electricity from within, shining out from between fanned platelets down the length of his back, and lighting up his forearms and forelegs from within. I catch his attention with an arrow, and he spews forth a burst of electricity in response, zapping a pillar right beside me before swelling into a crackling cloud of harmful toxins. The exterior of this arena is multileveled, with five or so ringed floors connected by staircases between them. I run down a few levels, and poking my head out into the open I notice that Kuromori has climbed up near my previous location, filling the upper floors with deadly electric gas. His glowing limbs are clear beacons, and I draw my bow. One shot to his front leg disconnects it from the wall, dangling, his whole body precarious now. A second shot lands true, and my foe tumbles to the bottom of his pail and lands squirming on his back. I scamper down the rest of the way and up onto his belly, the telltale blue glow of a sigil calling for my sword. I get a few stabs in before he rights himself, and I run back upstairs, climbing high to be sure I lure him far enough to create distance for his next fall. Like clockwork, I lure him up, shoot him down, and finish him off with just another two stabs. He rears up with my final blow, leaning into it before collapsing back to the ground, eyes extinguished.

Kuromori's battle is a clever cat-and-mouse dance of hiding, luring, positioning, and seizing the moment. It's also a battle inseparable from its arena, fitting perfectly with the colossus's unique attack and a means to expose its vulnerable underbelly—Kuromori is a lizard through and through.

And while this was a colossus that gave me trouble the first time I tackled him years ago, I remember exactly what to do now, with negligible time spent experimenting and improvising. I'm cold and effective, and the fight is over in only a few minutes. I've finally hit acceptance in my grief over these colossi, and in my numbness I've become ruthless.

• • • • • • • • •

Mono's ethereal voice in the white tunnel is almost audible now as I find my way back to the shrine somehow. Things are different this time, though, a break from the expected routine. A curious dream plays, grainy and skipping like worn-out film, a vision of Mono waking up on her altar, looking somehow different, darker. I'm ripped away from it just as quickly, back to Wander's reality, as Kuromori's statue shines, bursts, and crumbles. Wander wakes, looking more battle-worn than usual, and walks to Mono, putting a hand on her cheek.

# WHERE TREES
# NARY GROW

I RECENTLY HAD A MINOR EPIPHANY about what *Shadow* means to me. In large part, *Shadow* represents nature, the outdoors—a childhood spent exploring the fields of a summer home in Michigan, and the forests of a summer camp in Wisconsin. *Shadow* is the mystery in the woods—or rather *of* the woods—somewhere lonely where you can feel completely in the moment while being a part of something far bigger than yourself, something ancient. There's a certain danger, but also space for possibility and discovery. *Shadow* is a place of sylvan mysteries, turning over logs to watch tiny creatures scamper off into hidden burrows, or lifting up fallen leaves to find tiny mushrooms reaching up from a moist forest floor. It's far away from civilization, and its scenery evokes a spectrum of emotions that I don't otherwise encounter in my largely urban existence.

"I played a lot outdoors when I was a child," Ueda told me when I asked about his relationship with nature. "But now I'm more of an indoors person. What we call 'nature' is really a mass [a *katamari*, he calls it in Japanese] of information. Every time we have nature right in front of us, we're shocked at how much of this information is lacking in 'the natural things' expressed in video games." For all the sparsity of *Shadow*'s expanses, Team Ico did an amazing job of capturing just enough of that "information" as to provide a vital, if not totally realistic expression of nature. I find great comfort in that naturalist aesthetic, a fictional world that's beautiful in largely the same ways that the real world is beautiful. That same comfort is why I get distracted staring at the clouds while driving home from work, why walks around the neighborhood are at their most magical just as the sun is setting. These are moments that I can feel truly alone in, forgetting any stresses at hand while getting lost in the majesty of the cosmos.

• • • • • • • •

Riding west across the Forbidden Lands feels like riding into a storm, as clouds of dirt swirl high into the sky, blotting out the brightness that often pierces through the cloud cover. After a time, I reach the edges of a discolored basin of rock stretching off into the distance and across a winding crevasse.

This corner of the world is mineral and raw, powerful geysers of water intermittently erupting from the ground under darkened, misty skies. I find a smattering of trees near the mouth of a large cave just past the geysers from which my next foe soon emerges, his small but bright eyes shining out from a massive form in the shadows.

Basaran lumbers out of the cave, a gargantuan turtle colossus (unsurprisingly called the Turtle during development), propped up on strangely long legs that sprout straight out from its body before angling sharply back down towards the ground. He moves slowly but steadily, as a creature of such mass would. In a 2006 talk at the Game Developers Conference, Team Ico character animator Masanobu Tanaka spoke about the pursuit of realism in *Shadow*'s animation above all else, which was primarily driven by an attention to the colossi's perceived weight and energy levels. If the colossi were to move too quickly, they would feel weightless, expending an unrealistic amount of energy. This is also cited by Ueda as the reason that the colossi are different sizes, giving them the freedom to move at different speeds and therefore providing more variety. A similarly thoughtful approach is taken with Wander's animations, building in a slight delay before each jump (to crouch) or sword swing (to wind up). "We don't think responsiveness to a button means good control," Tanaka explained, unabashedly flying in the face of conventional wisdom.

Barasan's immense weight includes that of a broad, spiky shell that tapers off into a fiercely armored head, one that starts pelting Agro and I with bursts of electricity—a rapid and more deadly evolution of Kuromori's attack. I ride between Basaran's wide legs as he circles the barren basin, periodically rearing up before crashing down hard on the ground. He manages to nail us with an electric blast, a scary moment that sends Wander flying off of Agro as both tumble to the ground in a violent spill. Basaran is aggressive, a disgruntled giant awoken from a timeless slumber. And like the turtle he's patterned after, he has one reliable, characteristic weakness.

· · · · · · · ·

Ueda has spoken of his love for monster movies, and there's no doubt of their influence on *Shadow*'s stirring menagerie. The design of the colossi scratches a certain itch in my mind, a lifetime preoccupation with giant creatures. I've always loved images of whales shot from above the water, massive forms looming in shadow. I've had endless visions of towering monsters cresting the horizons of hills, city skylines, and oceans. I had a recurring dream when I was younger, set on a small island in an endless sea, with train tracks encircling the perimeter and a mountain in the middle. I sit atop the train, going around and around the island. In the distance, a Godzilla-like beast appears, slowly walking through the water towards the island. Every time I circle the mountain and my view becomes unobstructed, the beast is closer than the time before. The second it reaches the island, the dream ends.

• • • • • • • •

Basaran is imposing, but the visual clues throughout the arena help to inform my plan of attack. The geysers springing up from the battlefield every so often draw my eye towards his underside, and it's clear that I have to flip him onto his shell (a lesson also recently learned from Kuromori). I lure him over a momentarily stilled opening in the ground, and sure enough the geyser that shoots out knocks him sideways, so that he's balancing precariously on two feet. Thinking back to the bull colossus Quadratus, I plant two arrows in the exposed pads of Basaran's feet, and he comes tumbling the rest of the way down. I run as fast as I can around his huge kicking body, looking for something to grasp, until I spy the massive furry wall that is his stomach. I grab on and start to climb, and just as he starts to flip back over I crest the top, dropping onto his shell as he rights himself. From there, it's a reliable routine of making my way to his head (through valleys of rocky spines) and clinging on long enough to get a few good stabs in.

Basaran, betrayed by both his own lair and the obviousness of his design, remains nevertheless majestic in death. As much as I place value on Basaran's fate, though, the concern is not reciprocal—he wouldn't have thought twice about snuffing out my life, had I not bested him first. There's a terrible, age-old tension between the dispassionate enormity of nature and the very human impulse to conquer it.

# ITS GAZE IS UPON THEE

"GAMERS OF REDDIT," BEGAN A 2015 discussion thread, "what game do you think is a masterpiece of art?" Overwrought question aside, *Shadow* dominated the first page of responses. "After seven years," began another thread, "how is it that *Shadow of the Colossus* remains so unique?"

For an experience that resonates with me in a way that feels so personal, it's always odd to see the wider gaming community talk about what *Shadow* means to them. But I suppose that's true of all great art: We ascribe meaning and value to it within our own lives, and feel like it was created just for us. It's also a game that could only exist under the very specific circumstances of its release—a time when the only way to play console games was to buy them on discs and in stores rather than downloading them. And because they could be sold for $49.99 a copy, they could also be granted relatively large development budgets. Large publishers simply don't fund that scale of project for a new intellectual property anymore, at least not ones that are so distanced from commercially reliable gaming conventions.

Including an online multiplayer mode is one such convention, shoehorned into countless modern games to help round out a checklist of expected features and dissuade players from trading in a game as soon as they finish its main story (creating a commercially undesirable secondhand market). Perhaps ironically, *Shadow* was originally envisioned to be an online multiplayer game, a cooperative battle against a gauntlet of colossi. Back then, the project was called "Nico" (a portmanteau of the Japanese words for "two" and "Ico"), and you can even find an early concept trailer for it online—a group of horned riders can be seen taking down a large Quadratus-like bull colossus together. An idea of that scale was untenable at the time, and ended up as merely a stop along the way of development, but remains an interesting "What if?" It's also curious to see the massive worldwide success of the Monster Hunter franchise, a similar concept (of cooperatively fighting monsters online) that first launched a year before *Shadow*. Imagine a world with countless *Shadow of the Colossus* installments across every platform, each with a few new colossi and iterative features. Personally, I'd rather not.

• • • • • • •

While *Shadow* may have been scaled back on a macro level during development, the content never feels scant. And there's plenty to enjoy on the micro level as well—I'm having some genuinely funny interactions with the wildlife on the way to the tenth colossus. I go lizard-hunting for a while, scouring each save shrine I see, where some of the lizards find a way to elude me for *minutes on end*, despite only being able to hide in one of a few different spots. If I stand still, the lizards sometimes run right up next to me, but by the time I've readied my bow they're off again and out of sight. I'll turn the corner of a pillar and run headlong into a lizard heading the opposite way, startling both of us and spooking off my prey. Agro's been a real character recently too, reining up alongside me for no apparently reason, or charging off into the distance as soon as I look away. Riding aside a crevasse near the shrine, I leap from Agro to grab a hawk swooping low, and I catch it! Expecting a sightseeing trip across the landscape with my new friend, I instead weigh us both down, sinking into the crevasse until it eventually drops me to my death. (Though near the next colossus is a particularly large and special hawk—dubbed "Loki" by fans—able to support Wander's weight for an airborne tour for as long as he can hold on.)

Headed west from the shrine (where Wander is resurrected after death), I follow a circuitous route until I eventually spy the mouth of a cave on the opposite side of a valley. Inside, I find a wide sun-lit chamber, oddly filled with sand (we're still a ways away from the coast) and punctuated by a few stone columns and rock formations.

I ride Agro into this quiet place, and soon my foe makes his presence known. Dirge is a massive worm colossus, nicknamed Naga during development, after a being in the form of a great snake in Hindu and Buddhist mythology. He swims through the sands of this arena, patrolling it in wide arcs. Like Hydrus, Dirge is tough to get a good look at, beyond a long, ridged serpentine body with a few spines poking out. I ride Agro near his route, and suddenly it's a chase, one that I'm not fully prepared for as Dirge is *fast*— just as fast as Agro, if not faster—and aggressive. As he closes the distance between us he peeks out of the sand with huge owl-like orange eyes on an elongated face, before rearing up out of the sand, wide mouth agape and glowing from within. Dirge looks particularly innocent in some moments thanks to those eyes, but he's much less tolerant of my trespass than most other colossi have been, and seems to be actively trying to *eat* me. His attack knocks us over, almost killing Wander, and I scramble to mount Agro again before Dirge circles back to finish us off.

This fight is all about trusting Agro. She's both your means of escape and your offense, and you need to rely on her own sense of preservation to succeed. I lure Dirge out once more, but this time I spin the camera around to lock my focus on him, trusting Agro not to slam us into a wall or slow down. Up to this point, I've always felt protective of Agro in battle, but I've never asked her to protect *me* quite like this—to ride in a direction I can't see, and to be reliable in a way that's tough to expect from any creature, real or artificial.

It's an anxious moment, a massive beast charging towards me, spraying up sand in its wake as I struggle to keep my bow's reticule near Dirge's face as Agro's top-speed gallop keeps both of us shaking. Dirge surfaces to glare at me once again, seconds before attacking, and after a few haphazard arrows ricochet off of his face I land one successfully in his eye. He slams it shut, blinded, and I cut away at an angle from the path of his pursuit, letting Dirge continue straight into the cave wall. He crashes headfirst, ripping the length of him up out of the sand, and his writhing body gives me a brief window to stage a counterattack. I gallop back to him, dismount, and hustle up and across his furry back to a sigil near his head. I only get one stab in before he throws me off and burrows back underground, to start our routine all over again.

So much in *Shadow* is gained through repetition— not simply the act of repeating something for the sake or challenge of it, but rather to grant you opportunities for reflection, or to subtly change the context of a repeated action over time. This is effective on an emotional level, as much of your relationship with Agro is developed simply by spending time together—you can't very well walk the entirely of the Forbidden Lands yourself, but what starts as a working relationship evolves into true companionship. *Shadow* and *Ico* aren't the only noteworthy games to use time spent together as a means of cultivating an attachment—2007's *Portal* approached it more literally, giving players a Companion Cube to bring along to aid in their puzzle-solving, before (spoiler!) forcing them to destroy it near the end. The whip-smart comedic writing made the interactions soar, but it was the simple, repetitive act of dragging the Cube through your trials that created a meaningful attachment.

Visual and behavioral repetition is equally effective in *Shadow*—despite its wide and varied world, there's conscious repetition in the architectural design of the save shrines scattered about. Waking up at the Shrine of Worship after a battle, the same few things need to happen: You need to locate Agro, mount her saddle, find a spot of light to unsheathe your sword, and use it to locate the next destination. Other elements of your routine are incremented slightly over time: One more idol destroyed in the shrine, one more shadowy figure standing over Wander before he wakes, one more dove hanging out near Mono, one more beam of light piercing the sky. Your effect on the world is more overtly evident over time (as is the toll it's taking on Wander's increasingly darker, disheveled appearance), but it's up to the player to decide what to do with the information. Do you go right back into battle, continuing your increasingly unsettling mission? Do you let yourself get distracted and go exploring, just to buy time? Within the battles themselves, these same questions arise: Now knowing Dirge's weakness, do I simply exploit it again to finish him off? And what happens after I kill him, in those final moments?

· · · · · · · ·

Nick Fortugno is responsible for bringing the immensely popular *Diner Dash* into the world. He's also an adjunct professor at Parsons School of Design, where he teaches a class called Narrative & Dynamic Systems in which *Shadow* is prominently featured. "It was this indisputable line that was passed where I could point to something that was a tragedy in games," Fortugno tells me of *Shadow*'s narrative impact. "A tragedy in the sense of what we mean by a Greek tragedy—a story about someone whose tragic flaw leads them to make stupid decisions that destroy the world around them and eventually destroys them. And we are supposed to feel catharsis from that. [...] In a literal sense [and] in an Aristotelian sense, and I think that was an accomplishment for games. I don't think there are any games before [*Shadow*] that do that, or certainly don't do it as elegantly."

Fortugno also wrote an amazing essay for the Well Played series, called "Losing Your Grip: Futility and Dramatic Necessity in *Shadow of the Colossus*." Within it, he questions—as others have—whether the player agency inherent to video games undermines the drama used in more traditional non-interactive narratives and art forms. Using *Hamlet* as an example, he explains how if the play were instead a game, having control over the important parts of the story would eliminate the tension between the audience's desire and an inevitable outcome—a tension referred to as "dramatic necessity"—which would cause the story to lose its emotional power. Despite that conclusion, he argues that a similar dramatic power can still be achieved in games, through a trope that he dubs "futile interactivity," with *Shadow* as a shining example. This trope can be experienced most clearly after the cinematic death of each colossus, when the player is given back control only to be inescapably chased down and lanced by the tendrils. Fortugno explains, "By constructing interactive scenes where the player is led to believe that he can succeed when the goal is in fact mechanically impossible, the game uses multiple moments of futile interaction to give the tragedy its emotional power."

While the first time the tentacles kill Wander is a shock, the repetition of that experience and the eventual resignation of the player robs them of their agency, and gives them time to reflect on that moment. The scene will always end the same way, regardless of what the player tries to do, making good on the designer's intent rather than the player's objective. *Shadow* is an outstanding illustration of this trope, which has become an oft-used tool in providing memorable moments in modern blockbusters: the nuke scene in *Call of Duty 4:*

*Modern Warfare*, the microwave corridor crawl in *Metal Gear Solid 4: Guns of the Patriots*, even the (oft-maligned but narratively effective) "Press X to Jason" sequence in *Heavy Rain*. Striking moments of inevitability delivered in a way that only video games can, providing weight and consequence in the context of the larger experiences.

• • • • • • •

The second time I blind Dirge with an arrow, I'm ready for what comes next. I'm already driving Agro full speed toward him when he crashes into the wall, and something within me remembers how to stand up on Agro—an instinctual remnant from previous playthroughs—and I launch myself from that standing position high up onto the worm's thrashing body, and it's thrilling. I have more than enough time to finish him off, and he crashes lifelessly to the sand. Sometimes I try to celebrate the victory, but really I'm just proud that my skills at my favorite game have gotten better over time, not worse. But what does being "good" at *Shadow* say about me, several playthroughs in?

The tendrils find me particularly quickly this time.

# IT KEEPS THE
# FLAMES ALIVE

Celosia—called both Leo and the Lion during development—lies across the desert to the north, just east of the main bridge. Its lair is an enticing, hidden place, a temple at the bottom of a canyon that isn't visible until I'm right up against its precipice. Whereas most of the other colossus locales are wide arenas at the end of winding, secluded paths, this one is simply at the bottom of a hole in the desert. It's a surprise when the light of my sword points lower and lower in the earth as I ride closer, but it's far from the last surprise that this encounter holds.

• • • • • •

There's a fantastic Netflix documentary series called *Chef's Table* about world-renowned chefs and their differing philosophies towards food and life. The third episode focuses on Argentine chef Francis Mallmann, trained in French cooking but forever jet-setting across

South America, bringing rustic, almost primal cooking techniques to his restaurants. He cooks primarily with fire, from small wood-burning ovens to massive outdoor pits fueled by wood from the surrounding forest. The episode spends time at a tiny island home of his in the wilds of Patagonia, a stunning corner of the world surrounded by a misty lake, ringed by snowy mountains across the horizon. He talks about the elemental subtleties of cooking with fire, how it can be used on a full scale from one to ten, with every integer having a different property and application. He catches fish out of the lake, stuffs them with lemons, and bakes them inside a thick shell of clay that he dug out of the very same lake. It looks *insanely* delicious. Mallmann's connection with the elements is something that I strive for in the relatively little time I spend outdoors. I find myself deeply drawn to these open-air fantasies, of living off the land and blurring the line between my urban materialistic present and my agrarian ancestral past.

*Shadow* plays into these fantasies—I can gallop across wide-open spaces under the warmth of the sun, crunch leaves underfoot while creeping through hushed forests, all the while clinging to my magnificent horse. The yawning deserts of the game often bring about these feelings—less pastoral than the rest of the land, but even more majestic and remote. On the way to Celosia, I find a small burst of bright green palm fronds, a vibrant tropical contrast to their barren surroundings and a plant that I curiously haven't seen elsewhere in the game. And shuffling in the sand nearby… tortoises! Another creature that I haven't yet seen anywhere else. What a glorious little spot! The tortoises are smart enough to trundle around me when I stand in front of them, and when I step a foot up onto one's shell Wander tumbles over comically as the tortoise tries to walk away. It's a playful scene, and I again drift to wondering about its creator's intent. Why here? Why tortoises? Why make them smart enough to walk around me? Have they hung out with the turtle colossus Basaran before?

I rein up Agro at the edge of the desert hole that holds my enemy somewhere down below. Looking across the gap, there's a series of hairpin paths carved into the sheer wall of the canyon, which leads me precariously down to the bottom, leaving Agro to patrol far above. There's a small lake down here that I plop into, and not far from the shore, another sheer canyon wall with the mouth of a temple carved into it. Somewhere within, I can see heated air shimmering and a yellowish glow—a fire is burning, despite the loneliness of these lands. I climb in through a back entrance and head towards an empty room at the mouth of the temple, flanked by two burning braziers on each wall and a precipitous drop at the far end. As soon as I set foot within, Celosia reveals himself, leaping down from the rafters with a roar. He's a shockingly small colossus, roughly a tusked lion statue come to life, but with an intensity and hostility that simply can't be matched by the larger, more ponderous creatures.

The reveal of Celosia is a startling moment that I take for granted now, but in a game of escalating grandeur he's quite the anomaly at this point. Whereas the other colossi tend to serve as the levels themselves—which reminds me of the best marketing line for the game: "*Some mountains are scaled. Others are slain.*"—this eleventh encounter feels almost like a more traditional boss battle, while still building on *Shadow*'s efficacy at wordless instruction.

Celosia lunges at Wander, bludgeoning him unconscious, who then lies still on the ground for a few moments before being given the opportunity to stand up and run away. The closest hiding places are in the narrow gaps between each brazier and its adjacent wall. I climb up towards the flame at the top of a brazier, causing Celosia to charge its base. This knocks Wander off his feet, but more importantly it knocks a flaming torch down to the ground nearby—as shown through a brief cutscene, clearly telegraphing its importance. While there's no precedent for new items to interact with, I've been picking up fruits and lizard tails for hours, and I snatch the torch up off the ground. Celosia stops in his tracks, cowering from the flame—odd, for a guardian who "keeps the flames alive" as Dormin hinted—and slinks backward away from it step by step, ever closer to the drop at the far end of the room.

This is one of the more tense moments of the game, a strangely elemental dance. Fire can only be found in one other spot in the world (and there it's only decorative), and its rarity gives it power. The already small Celosia feels even smaller as he shrinks away timidly from the glow, though resting the torch even for an instant puts Celosia back in charge, swatting angrily at me.

I hang on, though, and we reach the edge as my torch begins to sputter. Celosia loses his footing and goes tumbling backwards, down to the bottom of the canyon far below, shattering his armor off in the fall and exposing a furry, vulnerable back as he lies dazed. From there, the objective from ten previous missions kicks in: *get to that fur*. I leap down after him, landing nearby (a better jump would have landed me *on* him), and I'm able to get a few stabs in while he's still dazed. Celosia regains his wits before I'm done, but from there it's just a matter of finding elevation, jumping onto his back, and finishing him off.

Celosia makes for a fairly complex fight, but *Shadow* leads me through it carefully, one action at a time. There's a great mixture of surprise, innovation, and familiarity to the encounter, a self-contained narrative arc that feels all the more intense and intimate due to its speed and scale. I'm not a flea on a giant anymore; I'm a lion tamer.

# A SILENT BEING
# WIELDS THUNDER

*SHADOW* IS MUCH MORE THAN just my favorite game—like other impactful art and media, it's helped to shape who I am. I always think of my favorite line from the (also formative) film *High Fidelity* (2000), spoken by John Cusack's character Rob Gordon: "...what *really* matters is what you like, not what you *are* like... books, records, films—these things matter. Call me shallow but it's the fuckin' truth..." I've long defined myself by the media that I love—I'm happy to be characterized by the movies and video games that I own, and I have no problem letting my iTunes collection speak for me. I'm much more than what's on my shelves, of course... but at the same time, I'm not. They serve as CliffsNotes of what I value in life, albeit through the intent and expression of others. I regularly wrestle with existential quandaries about what my own contributions to the world should be, if any (or if a fulfilled, happy life is enough to strive for on its own [or does true fulfillment come from a meaningful contribution to the world?]).

*Shadow* has become an integral part of my personal culture of inspiration, a creative palette to draw from as I find my own way through the world.

• • • • •

I awake in the shrine as always, Celosia defeated and the clue to my next target ringing in my ears:

"Thy next foe is…
Paradise floats upon the lake…
A silent being wields thunder…
A moving bridge to cross to higher ground."

Agro comes galloping up to me from somewhere outside the shrine. I hadn't thought about it until now, but where is she returning from? Is she just arriving back from where I last left her at the scene of battle, or has she been exploring the lands as Wander slept? How much time has passed? This simple decision to have her enter from offscreen each time, rather than already be standing next to Wander as he awakes, imbues the moment with mystery and a sense of momentum—there's no time for rest on this journey, and the moment you wake it's time to get moving again. It also subtly implies Agro's innocence in this quest—whatever mysterious forces bring Wander back to the temple each time, they are tied to his fate and burden alone.

Heading northeast across familiar territory, I scale a save shrine to the top and take in the best view yet of the striking main bridge—offhand, it's the largest object in any video game that I can think of, which makes it all the more impressive considering *Shadow*'s age (and Moore's Law). The bridge also grounds the scale of the other colossi; they're often huge, but would still pale before the bridge, access to which is restricted to all but those of a more human size, through the shrine beneath. Ueda often uses scale to great visual effect, something *Another World* creator Eric Chahi is particularly appreciative of, "Without the horse I felt like I had lead in my shoes, distances became infinite. I love the way Ueda stretches distances, how he plays with scale, and the emotions associated with that."

I head across a much lower land bridge and into an opening on a cliff face, which takes me deep into yet another shaded forest glade, buzzing with the sound of cicadas, as white butterflies dance between the trees. It's a perfect sort of place. Following a rough path back out up another cliffside path, it takes me to the mouth of a massive waterfall, bursting forth from the end of a wide lake flanked by carved stone columns. Forced to leave Agro, I scoot around a column and move deeper into the lake area, where I must swim to follow the light of my sword any further. After a time I find a set of ruins dotting the water, and pulling myself up onto one of the ruins triggers the introduction of my next foe. Pelagia stirs in the depths and crashes up through the surface, a bizarre creature with a mammalian body reminiscent of Quadratus or Phaedra, a shell similar to that of Basaran, and a massive armored face with no clear eyes, nose, or mouth, but anchored by two huge tusks.

Pelagia is an awe-inspiring, memorably specific colossus, and while intimidating, he isn't scary. Perhaps it's the lack of facial features or his graceful gait through the water. Though just as soon as his introduction is done, his tusks start buzzing with electricity and a substantial blast of energy is delivered in my direction as I dive into the water to escape. Curiously, his tusks glow blue and orange depending on his temperament, similar to the eyes of the other colossi. Ueda speaks to Pelagia's unique design in the art book: "This Colossus was called Poseidon. On top of its head are shapes that resemble teeth, but at first they were horns. There were also eyes in the beginning. During early development, I imagined the player using the bow to defeat it by shooting at its weak point." In the final version of the game, none of the colossi can be bested with Wander's bow—it's simply a tool, used for furthering some battles but never ending them. The deed has to be done with the sword, with the intimacy of steel into flesh—or what passingly resembles it—a visceral understanding of my actions.

The result of those visceral actions—giant creatures toppling over in the throes of death—lends *Shadow* some of its most memorable imagery, and also serves as the basis for its highest profile pop culture appearance: as a supporting plot device in the 2007 film *Reign Over Me*. The film is both drama and dark comedy, about a lapsed dentist named Charlie Fineman (played by Adam Sandler) who has lost his entire family in the 9/11 attacks on the World Trade Center, and his forgotten dental school roommate Alan Johnson (played by Don Cheadle) who tries to bring Charlie out of his shell. Charlie has receded from the world into his apartment, in denial that the tragedy ever happened, and spends much of his time watching old films and playing *Shadow*—a game about giant objects collapsing.

The visual metaphor is very much intentional, an inspired script suggestion by co-editor Jeremy Roush (who also had to sell the idea to director Mike Binder, Sandler, and ultimately Ueda for approval). Roush's father was a veteran of the Vietnam War, left mentally disabled by post-traumatic stress disorder and unable to work. To help pass the days, his father spent his time repeatedly watching *Aliens* (1986). Speaking to Kotaku in 2007, Roush explains, "*Aliens* is a thinly veiled kind of Vietnam veteran kind of story, and watching it is a way of thinking about it without telling yourself you are thinking about it. […] You could see where someone who was dealing with 9/11 would be engrossed by a giant that keeps collapsing over and over again." *Shadow* is featured in a few scenes, including a nice montage of Charlie teaching Alan how to play, one of the first times that Charlie opens up to him. "It's more like another dimension. You take a journey and discover yourself," Charlie explains. The montage ends with a thoughtful transition from footage of Avion's death to a beautiful real-life shot of a statue in a park, a mounted rider with a sword set against the sunrise of the following morning.

Whereas most films put about as much thought into what video game a character would be playing as what type of sandwich they would be eating, *Reign Over Me* integrates *Shadow* far more thoughtfully. As Kotaku's Brian Ashcraft puts it, "*Reign Over Me* must be one of the first Hollywood films, if not the first, to deal with games thematically and intelligently. While other industry pundits try to figure out how to take the latest blockbuster game and turn it into a movie or vice versa, *Reign Over Me* already has an insightful leg up: Let the games speak for themselves."

• • • • •

I swim through the arch of Pelagia's armpit and around him before scaling the grassy hills of his back up out of the water, huge waves spraying up as he thrashes, while I cling on with two fistfuls of fur. I reach the top of his grassy head, which is oddly flat, save for a broken rampart-like semicircle of the "teeth" that Ueda mentions (Poseidon's crown, as it were). I clang on one of the teeth with my sword and it reverberates like a tuning fork, sending Pelagia lumbering through the water in the direction the tooth was facing. It's a strangely subservient moment that contrasts with the dynamic that Wander typically shares with these wild and strong-willed creatures. It also rings of a fail-safe embedded in some of the colossi, and their exposed sigils. Why did their creator give these guardians a clear method of destruction?

I direct Pelagia to the two-story ruins nearby, and leap from his head across to the top level. I duck down behind a knob of stone that juts out of the middle as it's blasted with electricity. Pelagia has lost track of me, though, and he rises imposingly out of the water on his forearms to have a better look, huge cylindrical hooves crashing down nearby as his elbows bend. This exposes his furry chest, the blue light of a sigil glowing beneath, and suddenly I'm running and hurdling the gap between the ruins and Pelagia, landing dead center of the fur with my sword poised to strike. I get a couple of stabs in before he crashes down (destroying the ruins as he does so), forcing me to repeat the process by redirecting him to adjacent ruins before I attack his chest once again and finish him off. He rears up, pushing out a final rumbling roar before collapsing back into the water from which he emerged, waves spraying up to meet the inky blood that gushes from his wound.

I'm through three quarters of the colossi, and I can feel myself getting closer to resurrecting Mono, even amidst the grief and regret of what is now clearly a misguided mission. And I'm rewarded with a rare bit of the greater story in a cutscene before being taken back to Wander: Riders are coming. Several men on horseback rein up at the edge of a forest, led by the masked elder who spoke to Wander over a fire so long ago, warning him not to come to these lands. "Only a little more to go," he tells the other men, and in the distance they can see the tops of the stone structure that leads to the great bridge. While time feels endless and near-irrelevant in the Forbidden Lands, this revelation puts a subtle time pressure in place, a splinter in the mind of the player. Riders are coming, the thunder of inevitability. Are they coming to help you? To stop you?

# THOU ART NOT ALONE

Southwest across the plains, through a forest, at the end of a canyon trail lies a vast, blinding desert. A scattered few ruins dot the landscape, as do a series of strange half-buried stone rings (curiously the *only* objects in the game found to have been reused from *Ico*). It's a thirsty place, the air alive with sand particles, the bright horizon melting between sand and sky. And until my disturbance, there's absolutely nothing else happening there.

So much of *Shadow*'s appeal, its essence, can be laid at the feet of its "subtractive design," as Ueda calls it. Most commonly mentioned in the context of fine art—such as the paintings of Piet Mondrian—subtractive and minimalist design is an aesthetic in its heyday. It can be found in websites, architecture, industrial design, music, Apple products—basically everywhere. In *Shadow*, subtractive design was the process of cutting out everything inessential to the vision, leaving only that which was absolutely necessary. Whole gameplay mechanics were excised, huge swaths of the map trimmed off—if it didn't serve the central ideas and themes of the game, it didn't belong. Ueda elaborates in the art book:

> When I'm deciding whether or not to put something in the game, I'm always looking for meaning behind it, no matter what. Like, does it make sense to put smaller enemies in the game just so you can get items and experience points? I wouldn't have been able to forgive myself if I'd had a Colossus you wouldn't be able to beat without some item you'd get defeating smaller enemies. […] I had the idea of being able to warp through the use of an item, for example, but the huge field would have become pointless. There are two ideas central to the game: Colossi you have to climb and defeat, and an enormous field. I think that once we kept the overall consistency in mind, it was inevitable that the game would turn out like this.

Interestingly, many of these design lessons have become the norm in some circles of modern development, specifically in mobile games and in smaller-scale digital games on consoles and PC. Game development is more technologically approachable than it's ever been, and small or even solo studios have put out many of the more unique, memorable, *successful* games of the past decade. While *Minecraft* is a cultural juggernaut and exception to every rule, it was nevertheless created mostly by one person, and at its heart is a fairly simple experience. It gave players a toy box for crafting and creating in a 3D space, and became the Lego of the millennial generation. Mobile game blockbusters like *Flappy Bird* and *Crossy Road* are laser-focused on simple interactions of tapping or swiping, with an elegant learning curve and "just one more try" stickiness that feels skillful rather than exploitive.

Andy Nealen, an expert on minimalist design and an assistant professor of computer science and game design at New York University, regularly uses *Shadow* as a reference point in his classes. He's also the co-creator of *Osmos*, a serene puzzle game (and early App Store success) about colliding with smaller objects and avoiding larger ones in a visual Petri dish. Nealen tells me via e-mail, "Minimalism allows a designer to have a strong vision, but not describe it in every single detail, thus leaving the player to explore the elements, their connections, and their dynamical meaning. It also means only leaving the best parts in the design: If one part is better than the others, the others become a liability, and need to be removed or radically improved. The best designs and design processes I have witnessed have a 'cutting floor' that is ten times the size of the final game."

Naughty Dog's Neil Druckmann agrees, despite working on the other side of the coin—on massive blockbuster hits with a team of 200-plus people. While his studio's game *The Last of Us* is dense in world-building and action, it manages (like *Ico*) to tell a touching story about a growing bond between two strangers. Druckmann points to minimalism as his most effective tool. "It's paramount to making something great. It's easy to come up with a bunch of ideas and just kind of throw them in, and just get the player engaged on that, but to create something elegant… the question I always ask is, 'What are we trying to convey here and what's the least we need to do to convey that?' And we should do no more than that."

• • • •

I ride Agro through the perfectly empty desert towards a set of ruins that beckon the light of my sword. Stepping foot on them, I trigger the entrance of the thirteenth colossus, and a line of Dormin's clue returns to me: "A giant trail drifts through the sky…" Phalanx is the biggest colossus yet by far, a worm-like cousin of Hydrus and Dirge, though several times larger than both and with an even more alien face (possibly inspired by the dragon designs of the Panzer Dragoon series). Phalanx bursts forth from the sand, spiraling up into the sky, a bizarre but beautiful behemoth flying on a set of four long, narrow wings and supported by three sets of inflated air sacs on its underbelly. He's not here to attack, though— despite his war-mongering moniker, he's a gentle giant that will never once assault Wander. Especially at the start of this "battle," Phalanx simply flies a long, lazy path around the edge of the desert, undulating with the wind currents. I remember this battle well, though even if I didn't, the first steps to victory are clear. Phalanx's air sacs are ripe for the popping, and Wander carries an infinite supply of arrows. All three of my shots fly true, as the sacs wither and brown upon impact. Phalanx doesn't fall out of the sky entirely, instead dipping lower to the ground, the tips of his wings dragging in the sand as he continues to circle the desert nonplussed. Another clue of Dormin's flashes through my mind: "Thou art not alone." It's true—I'm far from alone, I have Agro. We have each other. Phalanx is still moving far too fast for me to catch up on foot, but atop Agro is a different story. I briefly watch my enemy's path, then I stir Agro into action, cutting across the desert to ride parallel to Phalanx's dragging wings as best I can, standing up on Agro's back in preparation for a jump. My angle is slightly off, though, and I'm on a collision course with a wing. I jump anyways, holding the grab button in the air… and I somehow catch the very edge of a wing, rather than the ladder-like handholds on its surface that I was aiming for. The momentum is too brisk to pull myself up, though, as Wander flaps in the wind like a rag doll. I'm not sure of my next move.

• • • •

Another inspired mind influenced by Ueda's subtractive design is that of Phil Fish, developer of the singular, world-turning puzzle adventure *Fez*. Fish was hugely affected by a post-mortem talk that Ueda gave on *Ico* years ago, in which Ueda discussed removing every superfluous element from the game. "After that lightbulb moment, I came at *Fez* with a hatchet, and removed tons of systems, features, and environments that didn't actually have anything to do with the core rotation mechanics or themes of the game. It almost became an addiction. It was liberating to axe huge portions of my game like that, knowing that it would let me focus on what mattered."

Ueda's central ideas of the colossi and the enormous field are the *entire* takeaway from the experience, only enhanced and given context by the game's sparse story. This focus also gives players the opportunity to fill the gaps in between, with just enough clues to stir the imagination without overtly explaining anything. "I think it's one reason why [Ueda's] games are set in dead worlds," Fish tells me. "You don't have to show this world at the height of its glory. You can imply so much with just… ruins. Small hints of what this place used to be—what it was about, were there people here? What did they look like? The story practically writes itself in the player's head."

Interestingly, the motivation at the heart of Ueda's focus on minimalism comes more from a desire to eschew current trends than a specific love for the style;

in that way, the current gaming market has dictated his aesthetic as much as anything else. As Ueda told me in an interview for 1UP.com in 2009, "It's my ideal to create a game that is unique. Therefore, if the market was full of games that had a minimalism, I would probably create games with excessive decoration and full of explanation."

• • • •

Phalanx pulls his wings up parallel with the ground, which allows me to hoist Wander up too, and make my way up the now-horizontal—though fully airborne— wing and hop over to the body. Phalanx's body is a wild, twisting landscape of its own, though it's simple enough to find my target: a furry patch containing a sigil on the wind-shielded side of a large dorsal fin that sprouts like a sail from Phalanx's back. I get a few stabs in before he stops tolerating me, but he doesn't attack like all the others, instead corkscrewing through the air before diving back down and burrowing fully under the sand again, throwing me off in the process. As I get to my feet, Agro is already running up to me, ready to go again. (What a pal!)

I track Phalanx with the light of my sword as he moves underground, and soon enough he ruptures forth for us to start our waltz once more. Killing the stubbornly peaceful Phalanx feels different from the others—an acknowledgment of sorts that Wander's quest is now fully evil, or at least terribly misguided. Wander is blinded by his desperation to bring Mono back, and his soul is rotting. And I as the player am slowly disconnecting from his selfish mission, watching as a second-person narrative becomes a third-person one.

# CITY BEYOND
# THE CHANNEL

WANDER WAKES IN THE SHRINE, another idol crumbled to ruins. One more dove flutters amongst many (thirteen, now), and one more column of light pierces the sky. Wander's complexion has grown pallid, dark lines climbing up from beneath his dirtied tunic and snaking across his neck onto his face, his hands and knees bloodied and bruised. As the colossi fall, so diminishes the spirit of Wander.

I ride long and far, snaking my way across both familiar ground and previously unseen canyons, eventually happening upon a series of small stone columns dotting an ancient path that leads to the mouth of a flooded cave. I'm forced to leave Agro there (a disappointment after our recent epic adventure together), swimming across and venturing deeper within, eventually emerging at the edge of a series of overgrown buildings—the remains of a small city, and the den of the next colossus.

•••

Earlier this year, I spent a Saturday afternoon hiking around San Francisco's Sutro Baths area with my girlfriend Amber and my good friend Ben. After an entire day and night of rain on Friday, the torrent subsided just enough to provide a misty veil for our journey, intertwined with a blanket of classic San Francisco fog. It was the perfect climate to experience that place, the overgrown ruins of what was once the world's largest indoor swimming establishment over a century ago, butting right up against the ocean (and now part of the Golden Gate National Recreation Area).

There's not much of it left beyond the aging cement walls of once-useful structures, embedded next to a swampy, eerily still lake that's only a low supporting wall and some rocks away from the churning waves of the sea. The area is flanked by very different, equally curious sights: On the south side, a hillside with yet more overgrown ruins, verdant carpets of grass and seaside mosses draped amongst them. On the north side, a stark rocky outcropping of cliffs breaking away from a misty forest, with a perfectly tunneled cave cutting through to the other side. Walking through the cave that day, we felt a heightened awareness of the density of the ocean, the moisture in the air, and the feeling that we were small and relatively new to that venerable place.

In that place, on that day, and in that moment, it *felt* like *Shadow*. The three of us reached this conclusion independently and easily. (It was also where I took the photo that adorns the cover of this book.) The collision of biomes, the vivid greenery clinging to wind-battered rocks, the horizonless sea in the distance—it all exuded a palpable air of mystery.

It's easy to ascribe specific moods or emotions to a favorite song or movie. But video games are different in that they're spaces to explore, and I've created countless physical memories from fictional locations. *Super Mario Bros.* changed moods completely when you went down that pipe into the second level, and the music, the color scheme, and even many of the enemies became tangibly cooler and subterranean. *Super Metroid* felt lonely because you *were* lonely—playing as a badass bounty hunter maybe, but spending hours on end trying to survive in uncaring and seemingly endless alien corridors. Even *Final Fantasy VII*, one of the first games to make me care about its story and characters, I best remember now for its locales and their atmosphere— the industrial depression of Midgar, the saccharine sheen of the Golden Saucer. Once games largely moved to 3D worlds, that relationship to the spaces within became that much more profound. I remember hiding in the nooks of *GoldenEye 007*'s Temple level, just out of view of my friends, and scurrying under obstacles to hide from the guards in the opening scene of *Metal Gear Solid*. *Crash Bandicoot, Tomb Raider, Halo*—or maybe *Uncharted, Gears of War, Call of Duty* if you're a few years younger than myself—the list goes on. Every gamer has their childhood worlds, spaces that at first felt foreign and exciting, then more familiar and comforting over time, maybe even nostalgic now.

*Shadow* is particularly adroit at building memorable spaces. While the world is large and naturalistic enough as to not feel set in its borders, or easily memorized, the colossi arenas are fully realized and more easily ingrained, as are dozens of other landmarks and scenes in between (many of which are intentional leftovers from unfinished arenas—part of the "noise" that Ueda left in). The ruins I now find myself in are one of those more memorable spaces, with tall symmetrical columns flanking single walls, overgrown stairways, and vaguely familiar arches and aqueducts. Soon enough, my quiet exploration of this hidden city is interrupted by its guardian, Cenobia (called Cerberus in development).

Somewhere between a boar and a large dog in appearance, Cenobia is another "small" colossus, roughly the same size as the lion Celosia but even more aggressive. Wreathed in armor—an ornate face mask juts out with tusk-like points of stone—Cenobia charges towards me on sight, and I instinctively clamber atop a fallen column to my left, placed by the designers as both the closest protective spot and a clever foreshadowing of the usefulness of fallen columns in this battle. I jump to an adjacent wall and climb higher, feeling safe for the moment, only to be thrown flailing to the ground as Cenobia rams into it angrily. I work my way back up before he can catch me, and venture even farther this time, climbing a tall ridged column near the end of the wall. Cenobia loses interest in me, so I launch an arrow his way and he rams the column angrily in response, sending it toppling over with Wander still on top. I'm scrambling again, just out of harm's way, and the fallen column gives me enough of a step up to reach the next low wall and the next ridged column. In this way, I work my way around the entire periphery of the ruins, column by fallen column, until we crash through a wall near where I first entered the city and into a crumbling courtyard beneath a cracked upper level above.

The scale of *Shadow* shifts dramatically with these smaller colossi, as the focus of each challenge changes over the course of the game. The first three colossi—Valus, Quadratus, and Gaius—are monolithic creatures in wide open spaces that Wander must simply find a way onto, followed by three that integrate their environment into that challenge—Phaedra, Avion, and Barba. The following three after that—Hydrus, Kuromori, and Basaran—incorporate more elemental attacks, and after those first nine all bets are off, as the game dishes out a wide variety of multi-step colossi, steadily building in complexity until the end. On the heels of Phalanx—the largest colossus, set in the most wide-open of spaces—Cenobia is a particularly conspicuous contrast, being one of the smallest colossi and set in a complex, intimate environment.

I'm running across the courtyard to climb to the upper level when Cenobia finally catches me with a blow, sending Wander sprawling. And before I can fully stand he hits me again—and again—until I'm close to death. I finally manage to dodge one of his blows, luring him back across the courtyard and putting several obstacles between us as I climb back around and above him. He charges the column supporting the upper level that I'm now on and it comes crashing down, shattering off much of his armor and exposing a sigil on his furry back. Without his armor, Cenobia appears much smaller, and the impact of his charges now dizzies him, giving me a moment to jump onto his back. The rest is a messy, violent affair, as Wander is sprayed with the black blood of this bucking beast as its life is drained away. He's become vulnerable as I've become savage, and the city shortly falls silent again.

There's a sadness in *Shadow*'s spaces, and as thrilling as they are to discover, they're emotionally taxing to return to. The site of That Horrible Thing I Did, a place to bear witness to the remains of a creature that was once sentient and is now another rocky mound amongst many, thanks to me. In this way, *Shadow*'s world becomes smaller just as quickly as it expands, the excitement of discovering a new area dashed by the realization that I probably won't return there.

# A GIANT HAS FALLEN

IT'S TRULY STRANGE THAT in an industry that borrows liberally from even the most minor successes, there have been so few attempts in copying *Shadow*'s formula in the decade since its release. Despite selling more than a million copies globally (and another million of the HD Collection), *Shadow* remains as singular as ever, perhaps even more so as the big-budget side of gaming has cohered into a series of predictable templates and formulas. I'm grateful for the independent-focused side of the industry, where innovation abounds, but even as a lifelong fan of a good blockbuster—be it games or movies—the big studio side of gaming rarely connects with me anymore. And it can't afford to even try, as the required development and marketing budgets to keep up with the neighbors are so astronomical that there's seemingly no business incentive to innovative, no reason to risk a player feeling too challenged to continue, mechanically or intellectually. Edges must be rounded off, character designs focus-tested into ubiquity, investors and retail buyers satisfied. With such inclusive ambitions, it's no surprise that it's difficult to find a means of personal connection in such uniform experiences. Often the best that we can hope for is a self-aware subversiveness (*Spec Ops: The Line*), or enough moment-to-moment choices as to allow the player a modicum of self-expression (*Far Cry 4*).

But even the best large development studios often don't have the leadership to focus on an idea as purely as Team Ico did with *Shadow*. I asked *Halo 3* game design lead Jaime Griesemer how trying to make something like *Shadow* would have gone over at Bungie, creators of the Halo series and *Destiny*: "It would immediately have gotten diluted. Someone would have said, 'We can't have a game where nobody talks, we're going to add cutscenes, we can't only have bosses, we've got to add this thing.' Because 90% of the team wouldn't have been on board. And at a studio like Bungie, there isn't somebody who can just say, 'This is what we're doing. Not that I don't *care* that you don't like it but it's not *relevant* that you don't like it,' and then everybody goes along with it anyway. You just see that so rarely, especially now that user testing is so popular."

From what I've been told about the project, *Shadow* was never once focus-tested. And to Sony's credit (reminder: my current employer, but these are the sorts of reasons that I work there), they are one of the few big publishers still putting out challenging games that aren't afraid to test players' patience as much as their mettle. *Bloodborne* is such a game, a spiritual successor to From Software's Souls series (*Demon's Souls, Dark*

*Souls I–III*), dark fantasy adventures with brutally unforgiving combat and terrifying, hostile worlds. It's one of the few mainstream(ish) series to have consciously and successfully taken cues from Team Ico, telling the bulk of its story through its gameplay rather than beating players over the head with it. So it's no surprise that series creator Hidetaka Miyazaki cites *Ico* as a key influence from early on in his career. Speaking to *The Guardian* earlier this year, Miyazaki talked about working at an IT company after graduation when some college friends showed him *Ico*. "That game awoke me to the possibilities of the medium. […] I wanted to make one myself." Within ten short years, he had become From Software's president (a feat unheard of in Japanese corporate culture), transforming the company into an industry leader.

On the other side of the fantasy adventure coin, games like *The Witcher 3* have become the standard, leaning heavily on lore and overt world-building, while overwhelming the player with places to go and things to do, so that nary a minute is spent exploring its stunningly crafted world without a task to accomplish. Ironically, even the unexplored spots on its massive world map are often announced with giant question marks ahead of time, minimizing opportunities for pure discovery. It's disappointingly pessimistic of game developers to assume that players won't have the attention span or curiosity to simply explore, instead leading them absolutely everywhere with a breadcrumb trail of objectives.

I don't mean to pick on *Witcher* (and I'm sure it won't mind my critique, as a huge critical and commercial success), but it's an all-too-appropriate example of just how different an approach so many modern mainstream games take to that of *Shadow*'s, despite surface similarities (third-person horse-riding monster-fighting fantasy game). Where *Witcher* has a wide upgradeable arsenal of weapons, *Shadow* has two (and the bow is more of a *tool*). Where *Witcher* has literally infinite enemies, across dozens of species of all shapes and sizes, *Shadow* has sixteen. Where *Witcher* has hundreds of storylines and sidequests, *Shadow* has one. Where *Witcher* has countless pages and conversations about the deep lore and history of its world and its denizens (a *450,000*-word script, in fact), *Shadow* has a few brief exchanges between mostly nameless entities. And yet even for a game that stars a supernatural detective (of sorts), *Witcher*'s sense of mystery still pales in comparison to even a few minutes of riding around *Shadow*'s empty expanses.

••

The fifteenth and penultimate colossus, Argus, guards an arena in a ruined castle in the far corner of the desert under the bridge. It's confusing to navigate, but I eventually crest a huge sand dune where the façade of the castle stands imposingly before me. (Agro completes the drama of the moment with a huge unprompted leap off the zenith of the dune.) Leaving Agro near its entrance I quietly explore inside, following a tall set of stairs up to a row of columns that gate one end of a long, rectangular arena. The arena feels man-made and meant for a duel, though any cheering onlookers are long absent. On either side are multi-leveled structures supported by more columns, two high bridges joining them across the top. While crumbling in spots, this castle is more modern and intact than most places in *Shadow*. The far end of the arena drops off sharply into a valley between mountains, and walking close to it triggers Argus's sudden entrance.

Pulling himself up over the edge with huge, brutish hands, Argus stands tall as the third member of the "Minotaur Siblings." Called Minotaur C during development, Argus is another anthropomorphic giant in the rough mold of the first colossus Valus and his bearded brother Barba. Argus stands apart most for his striking, expressive face mask—almost tribal in its design—and a stone mouth stretched wide across a fiercely furry head. He also carries a huge cleaver. After so many animal-like colossi, Argus feels fresh again, and while he may look like Valus, the complexity and challenge of this battle builds on many of the lessons learned since the start.

The fight with Argus is both a complicated puzzle and a knock-down, drag-out scrum. I run around his feet for a while before realizing that I need to make him stomp on a specific section of ground, raising it up high enough to allow me to climb up one of the multi-leveled structures—stadium stands, almost—along the edge. I catch his attention with a few arrows until he swings his cleaver at the structure, crumbling some of the platforms above me and allowing me to climb higher. I keep climbing until I'm near the top of the structure, crossing the bridge that joins it to the other side of the arena. Argus brings the bridge crashing down with a mighty swing, but not before I'm able to make a running jump towards him, landing on a soft shoulder. He thrashes about angrily, and I'm barely able to move before I'm thrown off. I finally realize that one of his weak points is a sigil on the hand that carries the cleaver, accessible only by triggering a small release point near the back of his arm. I make my way there (climbing back up the structure and hopping across to him for the $n$th time) and give it a stab, and finally he drops his weapon. From there I still have to position Wander at just the right distance from him (which is difficult, since he walks faster than Wander runs) so that he attacks with his hand, allowing me a moment to grab onto his palm and take out its sigil. And even after *that*, there's another sigil on his forehead that needs to be destroyed, and his thrashing only allows for a swipe or two before I'm thrown off and forced to scale him all over again. It takes me more than a dozen tries before I succeed, and by the end I'm just glad to be rid of Argus.

• •

My encounter with Argus is frustrating, fidgety, and if I'm being honest, not particularly enjoyable. The necessary steps felt a bit too opaque, too finicky in their execution. I'm reminded that *Shadow* can feel that way sometimes— even if you've figured out *what* to do, the same naturalism and looseness that adds a certain authenticity and makes for some beautifully improvised moments can conversely feel overly fussy, with an aggravating lack of precision. When you're a lifelong fan of something that's rough around the edges, it's easy to forget that its idiosyncrasies can be serious obstacles for those who haven't wholly embraced the experience. And as much as anything, *Shadow* is defined by its imperfections.

Still, it's interesting to think about what gaming culture would look like now had *Ico* been the definitive, chart-topping game of the fall of 2001—rather than *Grand Theft Auto III*'s criminal sandbox, released the following month—and *Shadow* the hotly-anticipated follow-up four years later. While *Ico* and *Shadow*'s legacies burn brightly amongst gaming intellectuals, both closely associated with the artistic aspirations of the medium, they're far from the mainstream cultural touchstone that *GTA3* and other chart-toppers became. But what if they weren't? What if more modern mainstream games were thematically considerate? What if they told the bulk of their stories through gameplay rather than cinematics, and let you truly explore a space? What if, sometimes, they traded explanations for mysteries, and trusted players to enjoy figuring out the solutions?

# MAKE HASTE, FOR
# TIME IS SHORT

WANDER LIES SURROUNDED BY SHADOWS, alone in a crowd.

"Finally, the last colossus…
The ritual is nearly over…
Thy wish is nearly granted…
But someone now stands to get in thy way…
Make haste, for time is short…"

Almost ten years later, this final quest isn't any easier to start. Difficult events lie ahead, and I've been putting it off for weeks.

I ride south across the plains, further than I have before, following the light of Wander's sword. I stop to check every save shrine along the way, hunting the last few lizards in hopes of delaying the inevitable. The world feels especially silent, an unseen energy drawing me towards a mountain range on the southernmost tip of the map. Lizards scatter across the plains and birds dance in the air above me, but beyond the ambient wildlife there's nothing else alive in this world except for Wander, Agro, and my final foe. I follow the sword's light to two closed stone doors embedded in the face of the mountain, between which a circular seal glows, spilling light onto a raised platform before it. I dismount, and standing on the platform I focus the light of Wander's sword directly into the glowing seal. The doors rumble and open away from me, strange synthesizers sounding, beckoning me beyond to the final encounter.

•

It feels lonely sometimes, having such an intensely personal attachment to a piece of art. While *Shadow* has affected so many others, no one can really understand what it means to *me*. Just as I can never understand what it means to them. Or for that matter, *anyone's* favorite *anything*. There's a chemistry, possibly even a spirituality, in connecting so deeply with someone else's creation. In many ways, I define my life by relentlessly sharing the things I love with the people I care about. But that may ultimately come from a selfish place. Maybe it's less about wanting others to experience the same magic and humanity that I felt, and more about wanting to be better understood in some small way.

•

There's a save shrine shortly down the path, and I rest at it for a time. I know what's coming, and the inevitability weighs heavily. Journeying on, I ride Agro up several sets of broad stone stairs to a landing at the top, overlooking a wide crevasse. The walls of a mountainous mesa extend up from temple ruins across the gap. The remains of a narrow stone bridge stand suspended in between, disconnected at either end but close enough for Agro to jump to. Coming up from the stairs, I continue Agro's momentum, riding her hard into a leap across the first gap, and she lands easily on the bridge. And then everything goes wrong. The camera spins 45 degrees to show the bridge collapsing behind us as Agro continues to gallop hard. She makes the second leap but the landing point is collapsing too, and in a heartbreaking moment, she understands the only option left, bucking Wander forwards to safety as the ground collapses under her. He's thrown violently to the ground and immediately leaps up to run back to Agro, but it's too late. A deft transition cuts between Wander running off-screen and the camera panning over the edge of the gap, as if to mirror Wander's view of Agro plummeting down alongside fallen chunks of the bridge, to a river far below. He yells for her, but she doesn't resurface. Wander hangs his head.

In all the deaths we've encountered so far, the loss of Wander's constant companion is hardest to take by far. Wander has sacrificed his humanity for Mono, but it's been his own cross to bear. Agro has been a vigilant, loyal accomplice, following Wander to the forbidden ends of the earth, but it's been Wander's decisions—my decisions—that have brought us to this. The loss of Agro is the most affecting scene that I've experienced in a game, the culmination of a body of wordless relationships and storytelling that began in *Ico*. The loss of Agro is a loss of innocence, a wake-up call to Wander that's come too late.

•

Wander stands up slowly and heavily, hands on his knees, before looking up to the distant top of the platform above where his enemy waits. I'm given back control, and there's nothing to do but keep going, climbing the ledges and ramps of the cliff face, higher and higher past precarious jumps and cubes of stone carved in strange patterns. Pulling Wander up onto a wide platform, the howling wind drops out, and all I hear are his footsteps. I run into a tunnel, up two staircases and back outside, and the air is humming with debris, wind whipping past visibly as a storm begins to churn above. Up a column and a few more ledges, Wander crests the top of the mesa, and rain is now spattering from skies swirling with darkness, a fitting introduction for the final colossus. His development name, Evis, is a curious one. As Ueda explains: "Because the game is focused on opposing a colossal force, we joked about it being anti-establishment. When you think 'anti-establishment,' you think 'rock.' And the god of rock is none other than… well, that was my train of thought when I spoofed a certain musician's name."

Our rock god, known to fans as Malus, stands towering on the far side of this arena, the most human of all colossi but rooted into the earth like a living statue. His long arms glow brightly around the wrist, cutting through the darkness as they crackle with orange electricity. From the waist down he's ringed in a complex series of platforms and ledges, several stories of dense architecture reaching all the way to the ground below. Far above, he looks out from the darkness with bright eyes set between devil horns, layers of protective armor cascading down his chest. Malus is the ultimate boss, a fittingly imposing finale to a game structured entirely around the "boss fight" convention. *Shadow*'s final boss fight makes good on the expectation that it will require all skills learned up to this point, and does so with the same purity that dictates so much of the game's design—there are no new moves to unlock, no button combinations to be memorized. There are simply the lessons learned from fifteen previous colossus battles, a relative lifetime of experience to draw from.

•

*Shadow* has been a constant inspiration in my personal and professional existence for the past decade, and I don't know whether writing this book will provide closure or simply deepen my attachment. I quit my job at EB Games in late 2006 and bought a one-way ticket to California with dreams of writing about video games for a living, endeavoring to show others what *Shadow* had shown me—that games could be not just art (duh) but *great* art, that they could trust their patrons to find their own meaning in the work. And now years later working with independent developers at Sony, *Shadow*'s artful, uncompromising spirit ever informs my own mission: to fight for games with equal heart and vision, that they may move and inspire others of their own.

•

Malus requires a harrowing approach, a desperate sprint across an explosive battlefield, dashing between low stone walls and ducking into trenches as he bombards Wander with deadly projectiles. An unnervingly subdued score plays throughout this battle, a slowly driving, rhythmic chanting of singers creating a gothic backdrop for Malus's imperial form. Looming high above, there's no deceiving this colossus, only staying behind cover as often as possible while zig-zagging towards him through the surrounding ruins. Missteps or moments of hesitation aren't tolerated, requiring split-second decision-making and perfect maneuvering. Climb, dash, duck, wait... sprint, roll, duck again. I have to wait for my health to return a few times, but eventually I work my way around across a narrow mountain ledge and through a series of underground tunnels, emerging from the ground beneath Malus. From there it's a treacherous climb up the scaffolding of his lower half, finding the right ledge to ascend or walkway to venture as Malus shifts beneath me like a skyscraper in the wind. Eventually I make it to his lower back, and find a cracked furry spot glowing blue, and a quick stab causes Malus to reach behind him to find the source of the annoyance. I leap from his back to his furry hand (with demonically pointed fingers), which he brings back in front of him in a massive swooping arc. He seems more inquisitive than enraged, and I'm able to right myself and run up his arm, stabbing another blue crack near his elbow and commanding the attention of his other hand. Again I leap across to it, and he holds it out in front of his face, simply curious, turning to look at the creature that dares encroach upon his majesty. I've barely had a chance to regain Wander's grip, and the next step is unclear, so I simply stab the hand I'm clinging to. Malus turns it upright and I'm able to stand, letting me recharge momentarily and giving me a window to draw my bow. I fire a few pointless arrows at Malus's face until I spot a furry shoulder nearby, and shift my focus. I land my next shot there, and he reaches over to tend to it, so I leap across to his shoulder as soon as I'm within range. Suddenly it all feels familiar, clinging to the top of the world with the Forbidden Lands stretched out before me as my foe writhes beneath Wander's feet, albeit under storming skies flashing bright with lightning.

I'm especially careful as I clamber onto Malus's glowing forehead, doing my best to avoid a precipitous fall, but the hard part is done.

My sword is driven home one final time as Malus groans in protest, holding a huge hand to his face as his life drains away and the strings kick in. He doesn't collapse to the ground, but rather sags in place, swaths of his exoskeleton cracking off as his massive arms hang limp. Just like all the others, his body is enveloped in shadow as the blue-black tendrils emerge to find me.

For a moment, there's nothing but death across the Forbidden Lands. I think of Agro.

# POOR UNGODLY SOUL

THE RIDERS HAVE ARRIVED, galloping hard across the span of the ancient bridge. The stone door of the shrine slides open for them, as it did for Wander and Agro so long ago. Swords and crossbows drawn, they enter, led by the masked elder whom they call Lord Emon. They walk down the cylindrical chamber and past the pool at the bottom, arriving just in time to see the final colossus idol light up from within before bursting in a bright flash and crumbling to the ground. They're too late.

The scene cuts back to the final battlefield, sunny skies shining over Malus's still form, now nothing more than an imposing statue. Wander lies still on the ground nearby, when he's slowly lifted into the air by an unseen force, his hand hanging limp as he's carried up.

Back in the shrine, Emon waves his hands over Mono, reciting a strange prayer, when a noise is heard and suddenly Wander is there with them, stirring on the floor. Shadowy figures climb out of the ground beside Wander as he wakes, looking much worse for wear—skin mottled with darkness, eyes glowing blue, small horns growing out from his head. Emon speaks to Wander, the truth of his words cutting deep: "I don't believe this… So it was you after all. Have you any idea what you've done?! Not only did you steal the sword and trespass upon this cursed land, you used the forbidden spell as well… To be reduced to such a sight… You were only being used."

Wanders stands, shuffling towards them. Emon's men walk towards Wander, drawing their weapons. "Eradicate the source of the evil. Look… He's possessed by the dead. Hurry up and do it!" One of the men launches an arrow into Wander's leg, bringing him to the ground as he grunts in pain, sounding strained and otherworldly as shadow seeps out from the wound. "It is better to put him out of his misery than to exist, cursed as he is." Another man raises a sword high with both hands, hesitating for a moment as he looks down at Wander, before bringing it down hard into his chest. Surprising them all, black, inky blood sprays up from the wound, like that of a colossus, as Wander stands unsteadily, gushing out darkness. Wander pulls the sword out before falling to the floor again, soon enough enveloped entirely in shadow. Mono lies still.

"You could call it 'sacrifice,' but I think it's closer to 'self-sacrifice'," Ueda says of the main theme behind *Shadow*, speaking to *EGM* in 2005. "That of the colossi, the main character, and even your horse, Agro. They all have to go through a great deal in order to achieve the final goal and bring life back to the girl. It's not an easy feeling to put into words."

Suddenly, Wander's shadowed body is growing, swelling into something huge and grotesque standing before them. Dormin, resurrected, given form. It speaks: "Thou severed Our body into sixteen segments for an eternity in order to seal away Our power... We, Dormin, have arisen anew... We have borrowed the body of this warrior..." The shadowy figures merge with Dormin's legs, as Emon yells to his men to place a seal over the entire shrine.

And so the truth of this quest is revealed, each colossus a manifestation, or perhaps a guardian, of these sixteen segments of Dormin, a great power that was banished to this land and torn apart. As the colossi fell and Wander took on their darkness and their burden, Dormin was inching closer to resurrection. It's a heartbreaking but perhaps inevitable result, the nobility of the quest long ceded to its desperation.

o

*Shadow*'s flurry of more traditional storytelling in its ending is a welcome bookend on an experience driven purely by the actions of its player. Its narrative form is steeped in the same mystery as its world, providing a space to ask questions and ponder explanations. According to NYU's Andy Nealen, *Shadow*'s unknowability will always be a part of its allure, "because we are humans and because we need nothing more in our lives than for things to be meaningful. Reducing the explicit exposition in the way *Shadow* does only helps amplify this desire. We simply like to interpret and project our own lives and values into everything we see, and when these match up—or not—we learn something new about ourselves and the world around us."

o

I'm given control of Dormin (and what's left of Wander, I suppose), the camera high above my back, looking down on a familiar space where I've woken so many times, Mono lying still even now. Dormin's body is darkened but translucent, with strange spindly legs branching off of it, dark fur around the edges, and fierce horns growing out from his head. For once, I'm granted the perspective of a colossus, but it feels slow and awkward, flailing my fists ineffectively as my faster assailants pepper me with arrows from below. I feel confused and vulnerable, hammering home the connection to the colossi I've been killing. Emon's soldiers grab Wander's discarded sword and retreat towards the entrance of the temple, past rows of fallen idols; I give chase, slowly, but I'm not even sure what I want anymore.

This is the first of two closing moments of futile interactivity, as Nick Fortugno calls them. The illusion of choice, or in this case *power*. I'm given a taste of the might of Dormin, the unwanted fruits of my labor, but in all this deception his ultimate objective isn't clear. He wanted to be free, but then what? The second moment comes soon enough. Emon and his men have climbed back up the spiral staircase, but Emon stops at the top, raising Wander's sword high before flinging it down into the pool below with an order: "Be gone foul beast!" The pool swells with light and power, whipping through the temple as Emon heads out towards the bridge. The power of the light from the pool sucks Dormin towards it, pulling the darkness out from within him as he struggles to fight it. He grows smaller and smaller until only Wander remains, enveloped in shadow, and I'm given back control.

I can see Mono lying ahead, wreathed in sunlight, but I'm tumbling backwards, white light swirling around me, pulling inexorably.

I can stand for a moment, pushing upstream towards Mono, but I'm swept off my feet.

I manage to grab the bottom of a staircase, holding on tight as the wind lifts Wander's body off the ground.

*Shadow* isn't just about self-sacrifice—it's about love, and hope. But more than anything, reinforced through its narrative, its primary gameplay mechanic, and in these final moments, *Shadow* is about holding on… and letting go.

"Just as [the player] learned fighting the colossi that one's mechanical grip cannot last forever," Fortugno writes, "so too do they realize that there is also a time when they must let go of the quest. When the player makes that decision, Wander does as well, finally giving up on his struggle, and allowing the healing of the game's end to occur."

I let go of the staircase, and Wander is pulled up and into the pool. The wind and the light go with him, and the shrine is silent once more.

Outside, the riders are crossing back over the bridge, but its support beams are swelling with light and disappearing, crumbling one after another as the entire massive structure collapses, the riders pushing hard to stay ahead of the destruction.

o

Mono lies still on her altar, sunlight flooding in. A long beat passes, and she stirs, eyes slowly fluttering open.

She sits up on one arm, looking around as if in a dream, then stands, her bare feet touching the cool stone floor of the temple.

She walks softly down the stairs, and looks up at the bright, silent hole in the ceiling.

She's interrupted by a whinny, turning to look as Agro limps into frame from somewhere outside the temple, one of her rear legs hanging useless, but otherwise intact. My heart aches as Agro stops in front of Mono, who reaches out to place a hand on Agro's broad face as they share a moment of sympathy, and perhaps a quiet celebration of life. The screen fades out to white before fading back into a flickering, sepia-toned shot of Valus's body, as the credits begin to roll. In this way, like an old film reel, I'm given a look at the body of each colossus in its resting place. A geyser bursts up behind the stilled shell of Basaran; the flame continues to burn near Celosia, its guardian even in death.

Even in its ending, *Shadow* never stops reveling in its quieter moments, something increasingly rare and valuable in a gaming culture that's often filled with noise and excess. Thatgamecompany's Jenova Chen knows something about pursuing those moments of quiet clarity. "When you have 100 singers in a choir group, it's hell to conduct and make sure everyone's on the same pitch so that singing can be crystal clear. […] When you reduce the number of singers it's a lot more likely that they can reach a perfect harmony, and so you can actually hear what the artist is trying to say. A lot of the AAA games, they put out big, epic opera—it's really impressive so at that point you're not really there to hear what they're trying to say, you're just there to be impressed by the formality and by the sheer scale of it."

o

Lord Emon and his riders make it across the bridge alive, stopping at the end to take in the dusty fallen rubble behind them. Emon looks towards the temple, remarking on Wander: "Poor ungodly soul… Now, no man shall ever trespass upon this place again. Should you be alive… If it's even possible to continue to exist in these sealed lands… One day, perhaps you will make atonement for what you've done."

Mono and Agro move slowly down the hallway of fallen idols, Agro pushing through the pain of her limp. They walk to the pool at the end, now empty... save for a small baby lying at the bottom, perfectly human and naked except for two small horns protruding from its head. Mono picks it up and it gesticulates in her arms, burbling with baby noises—not upset, just new to this world. Reborn. (I can make the baby wiggle and cry out on command by pressing various buttons, controlling Wander in yet a third form.)

Much has been speculated on the connection between *Shadow* and *Ico*, from their game worlds to their stories. Is the reborn Wander the progenitor of a long line of horned children, cast out from their villages like Ico due to a fear that they might rise to great power? Is *Ico*'s queen sacrificing the children to collect residual traces of Dormin? The HD Collection presents the only tangible bridge between them—as you select a game from the menu, the view quickly pans across a long, interconnected piece of artwork, across a wide ocean in between the two worlds. Ueda has confirmed that they exist in the same world, but beyond that—as with everything in *Shadow*—it's more fun to wonder and speculate. I asked producer Kyle Shubel about the culture of mystery around the game: "Most mystery games walk you through a series of puzzles and then give you an answer. The reason why *Shadow* still lingers is that they never gave you the answers... There are mysteries in *Shadow* that are left intentionally unspoken. If you ask a question enough times and you eventually get an answer, it's no longer a question."

*Shadow of the Colossus* is the great mystery of the woods, a sweeping dream of giants and the tragic circumstances of their downfall. It's an expression of love in art, wordless companionships forged under difficult conditions. It trades on trust, and spaces to explore, and the curiosity that engenders. And beyond being a transcendent, important work of art, it's an essential chamber in the emotional heart of an entire medium.

o

Agro leads Mono and their newborn companion up the spiraling path next to the pool, out through the recently opened stone door at the top, and past the point where the bridge fell—up a ramp to a garden hidden at the top of the shrine. It's a beautiful, peaceful, sun-dappled place. A fawn appears in a clearing and walks over to greet them, ears twitching. A chipmunk emerges, equally curious about these strange new guests. White doves land too, a brown hawk among them. After a few moments the hawk departs, flying up and away as the camera follows, leaving everyone else behind— away from the temple, away from everything, into the blinding sky above. The weather and time of day shift as the hawk flies, time flowing in this place once again. Just as it began, *Shadow* ends on the wings of a bird.

# EPILOGUE

IN ALL THESE YEARS SPENT with *Shadow*, one great mystery has ever eluded me: a visit to the garden that lies above the Shrine of Worship, otherwise seen only briefly in the game's closing cutscene. With enough stamina, you can scale a mossy path all the way up the side of the shrine and visit the secret garden within the game itself. While *Shadow*'s original release contained an exploitable glitch whereby players could cheat their way to the top from the get-go, I always felt that I had to earn it legitimately. While the path one must climb is very specific, there's no great trick to it beyond being able to hang on for the few minutes it requires—every colossus felled and lizard tail gathered extends Wander's stamina bar slightly, and after three full playthroughs (through which stamina gained carries over) I was finally equipped for the ascent.

For all its subtractive focus, even *Shadow* falls prey to some gaming conventions, features designed to extend the experience beyond a single playthrough of its story. Hard Mode, in which colossus attacks do more damage and some colossi bear extra sigils to be found and destroyed, and Time Attack, in which players can unlock special items (such as stronger swords and a cloak of invisibility) by defeating the colossi under specific par times. These extras stand in stark contrast to the spirit of the main game, and I've never had particular interest in exploring them. But the secret garden is something different—part and parcel with the cryptic lifeblood that pumps through the veins of Team Ico's entire body of work.

Starting from a vein of moss growing on the shadowed eastern side of the shrine, I climb straight up, making large two-handed leaps to cover as much distance as possible using relatively little stamina. I climb up as high as I can, before being forced to shimmy across a horizontal ledge, down another wall, across another ledge, and then past one more set of each before a final ascent up a long, hanging column of stone. There's no place to rest along the way, and I crest the top with the very last pink pixel of my stamina slipping away. In some ways the shrine itself feels like the ultimate colossus, an ancient, implacable obstacle.

I stand on a walkway outside of the door that Agro and Wander first entered in the opening cutscene so many playthroughs ago, the massive length of the central bridge stretching off into the distance ahead of me, *away* from the shrine. Before heading up an adjacent ramp to the garden, I run back down the entire length of the bridge, just to experience the Forbidden Lands from stunning new heights, alone except for the sounds of Wander's footsteps and the howling wind. And Agro, of course—infallible, unyielding Agro— running astride far below, her detail so obscured that she's indistinguishable from one of the skittering black lizards. Soon enough even the wind drops out, and in the near-silence I feel as if I'm pushing *Shadow's* world to its limits, asking it to show me things that it only half-intended, the reward for a challenge it never expected me to complete. At the very end of the bridge—ten minutes of running later—an ornate temple entryway is presented, but a fierce wind blows Wander back from its opening.

I run all the way back, this time taking the ramp up towards the garden, through a shadowed corridor. And suddenly I'm standing where Mono, Agro, and a reborn Wander gathered in a cutscene relative moments ago, at the precipice of the last great mystery, the final unturned stone in a decade of exploring. It's a serene place, dotted with yawning arches and trickling waterways, with further architecture stretching high above in countless other inaccessible levels of the shrine. The garden is also more verdant than most areas, as large fruit trees sprout throughout, dripping with a very curious type of fruit— one that permanently *reduces* your life bar and stamina when eaten. When I asked Ueda about this in a 2009 interview for 1UP.com, his answer was equally curious: "The fruit in the ancient land was set to get you closer to non-human existence. The [secret garden's] fruit was set to return you to a human one."

There's both an odd satisfaction and an unsurprising sadness in exploring this final niche of the world, the closing notes of an epilogue that I had all but given up on seeing. Without tangible reward, the secret garden is a perfect distillation of *Shadow*—beauty for beauty's sake, a journey more important than its destination.

There's perhaps a more surprising feeling, though, in accomplishing the climb, running the span of the bridge, and finally visiting the garden. Not quite disappointment or regret, but something closer to the feeling of growing older—there's forever a little less mystery and magic in the world now, and I can never turn that final stone back over. Getting to the garden was exciting, but well, having never gotten there was even better.

# NOTES

I had four tabs open in a browser window throughout most of this project: the hugely informative Team Ico Wiki (http://bit. ly/1PJGpyd); Aria "GlitterBerri" Tanner's Game Translations site in which she generously translates the Japan-only *Shadow* art book (which I quote from liberally) and much more (http://bit.ly/1H3FuHy); Nomad's blog, the greatest *Shadow* information rabbit hole of them all (http://bit.ly/1kY8INS); and Emanuele "Emalord" Bresciani's Electric Blue Skies, a site dedicated to beautiful in-game photography that I often used for visual reference (http://bit.ly/1kzi2rJ).

The version of the game used for this playthrough was *The Ico & Shadow of the Colossus Collection* (2011) for PS3 (which can actually be played in 3D as well—it's pretty sweet). It also contains some nice extras, including two developer interview videos which I quote from: "Walking with Giants" and "Walking in the Footsteps of Giants" (in which Ueda explains the inspiration for *Ico*, and Jinji Horagai talks about playing their own rock 'n' roll).

In rough order that you read them, my other sources:

Ueda speaking about his experience with *Super Mario Bros.* comes from an article on 1UP.com called "The Man Behind

Ico, Shadow of the Colossus, and The Last Guardian"
(2011), written by my old colleague Matt Leone (http://bit.
ly/1NyH5SA).

That great *Ico* quote from Ollie Barder comes from "A break
from the norm" (2005) (http://bit.ly/1WUMdKZ). The first
Neill Druckmann quote comes from "How Ico Informed The
Last of Us" (2013) by Rob Crossley (http://bit.ly/1Pv3TIT).
*Official PlayStation 2 Magazine UK* ran an interview with
Ueda (2002) that I found transcribed on a blog called Cats
Under a Tree, in which I learned that *Ico*'s concept was partially
inspired by *Galaxy Express 999*, its theme by Scarborough
Fair, and its architecture by the work of Giovanni Battista
Piranesi (http://bit.ly/1Lh7XVe).

Ueda's description of the objects he combined to create the
colossi design comes from "Giant Steps" (2005, Issue 97) in
*Official U.S. Playstation Magazine*.

The fan names for the colossi seem to originate on a
PlayStation Forums thread (2005), found here: http://bit.
ly/1kzipTf.

Kenji Kaido's quote about *Shadow* coming from the heart
is from an interview in the December 2005 issue of *Weekly
Famitsu*, translated and posted by GlitterBerri of course:
http://bit.ly/1N5NhXK

Bryan Ma's "Ueda and A Boy and His Blob and A Girl
and A Horse" (2009) can be found on his blog (http://bit.
ly/1Lh8wyq). I changed the sex of Epona and Agro while
quoting him, since he incorrectly refers to both of them as

male (which is not really his fault in the case of Agro, since the English release of *Shadow* also gets it wrong).

My great-uncle's touching, fascinating obituary (2004) can be found on The Independent (http://bit.ly/1Sv65hk).

Shmupulations transcribed (and/or translated?) the Great Scene Sharing event that took place in 2011, where Ueda and Keiichiro Toyama (*Silent Hill, Siren, Gravity Rush*) interviewed each other (http://bit.ly/1B7q0vE). This is where the Ueda quote about first adding sad music to the battles comes from.

"The quest for Shadow of the Colossus' last big secret" (2013) by Craig Owens can be found on Eurogamer (http://bit.ly/1SoWidB).

The Ueda quote about the Minus World in *Super Mario Bros.* comes from "An Audience With… Fumito Ueda," a killer interview by Daniel Robson found in Edge Magazine (2013, Issue 261).

Nick Fortugno's "Losing Your Grip: Futility and Dramatic Necessity in Shadow of the Colossus" (2009) is worth reading in its entirety (http://bit.ly/20VMQnf).

Brian Ashcraft's Kotaku article on *Shadow*'s appearance in *Reign Over Me*—"The Colossus and the Comedian" (2007)—can be found here: http://bit.ly/1HNFH1K.

Oh hey, I get to cite myself! Check out my "Shadow of the Colossus Postmortem Interview" (2009) with Ueda on 1UP, several choice quotes from which are used throughout the book: http://bit.ly/1X1hsir

Simon Parkin's interview for *The Guardian* with *Bloodborne* creator Hidetaka Miyazaki (2015)—in which he speaks about being awoken to the possibilities of the medium by *Ico*—is right here: http://bit.ly/1GJG22r

Another friend and colleague, Shane Bettenhausen, interviewed Ueda in *Electronic Gaming Monthly* (2005, Issue 198) for "Afterthoughts: Shadow of the Colossus," in which he stated that self-sacrifice is the main theme of *Shadow*.

# ACKNOWLEDGEMENTS

Thanks foremost to Amber Cox for her boundless encouragement, support, and love over nine months of evenings and weekends spent writing, and for understanding how important this was for me to do. I would travel to forbidden lands and trust mysterious voices for you.

Thanks to Jess Suttner for a lifetime of brotherly encouragement (and more recently, great feedback), and to our parents Linton Suttner and Shelley Davis for imbuing us with an appreciation for art and culture that lets us divine our way through the world.

Endless thanks to Gabe Durham for seeing something in my pitch and helping to shape my drafts into something just-maybe-worthy of his amazing series. And to Michael P. Williams for being the goddamn Batman of researchers and giving me reams of helpful/hilarious/thoughtful feedback. That guy should write a book.

This definitely couldn't have happened without Dan Sutter, Ben Sutter, and Matt Milkowski, who understand my love for *Shadow* like few others and who all spent an inordinate amount of time making sure that this book was true to that love. And also to Tom Mc Shea, Scott Hannan, and Doug Wilson for key moments of support/feedback/friendship.

Thanks to Michael "Nomad" Lambert for his openness, feedback, and downright incredible documentation of *Shadow*.

Huge thanks to my many inspiring, generous, brilliant interview subjects: Eric Chahi, Jenova Chen, Neil Druckmann, Kyle Shubel, Jaime Griesemer, Adam Saltsman, Andy Nealen, Craig Adams (double thanks for the great foreword!), Nick Fortugno, Vander Caballero, Nels Anderson, Phil Fish, Michael "Nomad" Lambert, John Davison, Allan Becker, Josef Fares, Tameem Antoniades, Marty O'Donnell, Greg Off, Nao Higo, Rich Siegel, the Acid Nerve team (Mark Foster + David Fenn), and the Sunhead Games team (Lee-Kuo Chen + Chia-Yu Chen). I'm sorry that I couldn't include more of your insights, but they will eventually live at http://shadowbookextras.tumblr.com.

Thanks to current and former colleagues throughout the gaming industry for encouraging me to do my thing and for helping to challenge the status quo.

Miscellaneous but important thanks to Ryan Plummer, Joseph M. Owens, Adam Robinson, Ryan Payton, Ophir Lupu, Jennifer Clark, Scott Rohde, Shuhei Yoshida, Adam Boyes, Gio Corsi, Mena Sato, Kevin Chung, Alyssa Casella, Mark MacDonald, Greg Off, Shane Bettenhausen, Dan "Shoe" Hsu, Paul McGuire, and Loretta Oleck. And to Scrivener for being awesome writing software.

Bonus thanks to Derek Yu for making *Spelunky*, my second-favorite game and the one that made me take notice of Boss Fight Books in the first place.

And lastly, eternal thanks to Fumito Ueda for letting me interview him twice (six years apart), and for making a piece of art that changed my life. I'm ever in your shadow.

# SPECIAL THANKS

For making our second season of books possible, Boss Fight Books would like to thank Ken Durham, Jakub Koziol, Cathy Durham, Maxwell Neely-Cohen, Adrian Purser, Kevin John Harty, Gustav Wedholm, Theodore Fox, Anders Ekermo, Jim Fasoline, Mohammed Taher, Joe Murray, Ethan Storeng, Bill Barksdale, Max Symmes, Philip J. Reed, Robert Bowling, Jason Morales, Keith Charles, and Asher Henderson.

# ALSO FROM
# BOSS FIGHT BOOKS